Rethinking Education in The Hills of Northeast India

Rethinking Education in The Hills of Northeast India
(Case of Manipur)

Edited by

A.S. Yaruingam

A.C. Kharingpam

SHIPRA

Rs. 695; US$ 35.00

ISBN: 978-81-7541-787-8

First Published in India in 2015

Rethinking Education in the Hills of Northeast India—Case of Manipur

Published by:
SHIPRA PUBLICATIONS
LG 18-19, Pankaj Central Market, I.P. Ext.
Patparganj, Delhi-110092
Tel: 91-11-2223 5152, 2223 6152
E-mail: info@shiprapublication.com
www.shiprapublication.com

Preface

Education promotes economic growth, national productivity and innovation, and values of democracy and social cohesion. Realizing this very fact, two of the millennium development goals (MDG) pertain to education, these two goals are – one, universal completion of primary schooling and two, gender parity in primary and secondary schooling.

Investment in education benefits the individual, society, and the world as a whole. Broad based education of good quality is among the most powerful instrument to reduce poverty and inequality. With proven benefits for personal health, it also strengthens nation's economic health by laying the foundation for sustained economic growth.

It is commonly known fact that countries with higher primary schooling and a smaller gap between boys and girls schooling tend to enjoy greater democracy. Education also engenders to provide more peace and security to human life. It enhances natural resource management and national capacity for disaster prevention and adoption of new environment friendly technologies.

Women with formal education are more likely to use reliable family planning methods, seek medical care, ensure their children are immunized, be better informed about nutritional requirements and adopt improved sanitation practices. As a result their infants have higher survival rates and to be healthier.

Education, in a sense, is the mother of all round human development.

Formal education in tribal belts of Manipur came towards the end of 19th century through Christian missionaries. This was followed by introduction of schools in districts and villages by the government. People started receiving the fruits of education—improving their economic life and changing their outlook and global views. Today, tribal people are highly conscious of education as it has been the basis of transforming their individual and societal life.

However, the present scenario of education in the districts of Manipur is not that encouraging. Government Schools seem to have negative consequences with multiple ramifications. As a consequence of deterioration of government schools, private schools which charge higher school-fees are mushrooming in the tribal districts. This has brought to unbearable hardships to the parents in the villages, apart from deteriorating the scope and standard of education.

To give new thoughts and a direction to this problem, the Tangkhul Scholars' Association (TSA) organized a two-day national seminar 'Rethinking Education in Tribal Districts of Manipur' at Ukhrul and deliberated on these issues of the region.

The editors expressed their thanks to the contributors for their meaningful contribution without which this book won't have been possible. Thanks to Shipra Publications for their excellent work.

A.S. Yaruingam
A.C. Kharingpam

Contents

Preface v

1. Introduction 1
A.S. Yaruingam

2. Pettigrew's Children: History of Print Culture of Tangkhul Language 15
A.S. Shimreiwung

3. Colonial Ideology and the Early 20th Century Texts: An Overview of Hegemony in the School Texts of Manipur 33
A.C. Kharingpam

4. Bankruptcy of Education: Ideology and Literature in the Context of Tangkhul Society 43
Yuimirin Kapai

5. Traditional Knowledge, Social-cultural Practices and Modern Education 64
Tuisem Ngakang

6. Curricula and Education System of Manipur State 76
Ringkahao Horam

7. Tangkhul-Naga Grammar: A Study of Word Formation 87
Victor Ahum

8. Social Enquiry of Educational Scenario: The Mapithel (Pesii) Range of Ukhrul District, Manipur 101
Mes Jajo, Lucy Jajo and *Maheishang Awungshi*

9. Education and Spirituality in the Present Context 111
R. Wonkhuimi

10. Women Education and its Potential of Harnessing Sustainable Handloom Industry in Northeast 119
Lucy Jajo Shimray

11. Right to Education (RTE) Act 2009: Its Relevance in Manipur 140
Thothuingam Shinglai

12. Education and Identity Formation: Some Reflections on the History of the Nagas of Chandel District (With Special Reference to the Monsang Nagas) 156
W. Somie Monsang

13. Traditional Forest Management through Indigenous Knowledge and Practices in Northeast India: A Case Study in Tangkhul Community, Manipur 170
Franky Varah and *T. Shimrah*

Contributors 192

Introduction

A.S. Yaruingam

"Plants are developed by cultivation and men by education".
—*John Locke*

Several thinkers have defined education in different ways giving different meaning in the context they dealt with. Western philosophers like John Locke said, "Plants are developed by cultivation and men by education." This means education is a means and process for the development of men. According to John Dewey, education is 'not a preparation for life, rather it is the living'. Education is the process of living through a continuous reconstruction of experiences. It is the development of all those capacities in the individual, which will enable him to dominate over the environment and fulfil his possibilities'.

According to Mahatma Gandhi, education is "drawing out the best in man-body, mind and spirit". To Rabindranath Tagore, 'Education enables the mind to find out the ultimate truth, which gives us the wealth of inner light and love and gives significance to life.' Gandhi and Tagore, who were more or less humanists and philosophers, viewed education in a more abstract terms emphasizing on the spiritual-moral aspects. Mrs. Indira Gandhi, who was a practising politician, who had confronted with ground reality of Indian society, defined education in more pragmatic term. According to her, 'Education is a liberating force and in our age, it is also a democratizing force, cutting across the barriers of caste and class, smoothing out inequalities imposed by birth and other circumstances' (Parankimli, 2012).

The ubiquitous Chinese maxim, which says, 'If you plan for one year, cultivate rice, if you plan for ten years, plant a tree, but if you plan for hundred years, educate the people' expresses what education means for the Chinese.

If we examine each of the definitions given above, they all talk about the development of a person to the optimum level possible so as to be a better and more effective being. Therefore, education is not just acquiring skill of reading, writing and collecting information, rather it is a process of moulding a person to be a better being, to be more civilized, have etiquette in behaviour, be productive and useful to society, who could ultimately bring positive transformation in the society at large. It is in this context that a writer wrote, 'Education can turn over population, which has become a liability to the society, as assets' (Patil, 2012).

The importance of education for all round social, economic and political development is needless question to ask. Education is the fundamental requirement for progress and development. Studies done by researchers have clearly confirmed that there is inseparable co-relation between the rate of literacy and level of economic development. President Pranab Mukherjee in his address to participants of the 'School Chale Hum Abhiyan' on 28 June 2014, in Odisha said, "Education is the most efficacious instrument for transforming a society. It broadens perceptions and gives individuals better insights into the diverse aspects of their life. Education not only brings about personal evolution and growth, but also brings progress and positive development of the people."

Education empowers an individual by keeping him aware of the given surrounding as well as the rules and regulations of the society. It's only when a person is fully equipped with knowledge that he can be an effective citizen of a nation and be able to question the authority for its negligence or discrepancies. It is also true that people can bring about development only when they know where improvement is necessary for the greater good of mankind. Over all, education helps us to understand oneself and realize an individual's potential and qualities as a human being. Those, who have got the right kind of education, steer the path of development and progress for their country. It is these individuals, who go ahead and become scientists, inventors, entrepreneur and politicians, who work together to form the very backbone of the society. On the other hand, if a nation does not equip its citizens with proper intellect, the economic and social framework of the nation crumples and falls, paving the way for anarchy, degradation, and violence. Our present society seems to be falling under this syndrome.

From sociological perspective, education is taken as a channel for transmitting the cultural heritage to the new generations. But in this fast changing society, where things keep on changing from generation to generation, the educational system in such a society is not only to transmit the cultural heritage, but also aid in preparing the young for adjustment to any changes'. And thus education system is expected to perform a new and different role in modern society (Patil, 2012).

It is a known fact that equipping beaming youths with the right kind of skill and knowledge brings development and prosperity to the nation. In this regard, South Korea's experience is one of the most appropriate cases. South Korea's economy was completely in a state of shambles. After the Japanese left the country, the second President, General Park Chung-hee, realized the need of education to bring out the nation from such an abysmal situation. He made massive investment in the education sector. Education system was reformed making its methods of teaching and curriculum relevant to the practical needs of the people. The cost of education was made affordable to every citizen and made compulsory for all children (Kim, 2012). Since then, the Korean phrase '*kyoyukyol*' meaning 'Korean's zeal for education' became the pet word for South Koreans (Seth, 2012). Comparatively, South Korea has lesser natural resources than other Asian countries, such as India. The sole economic asset that nature endowed to Korea is 'Ching Sen' (a type of herb) and the Hangkang river, which passes through the middle of the Seoul city that facilitates trade and commerce. But today Korea stands at 9th rank in the economic development index of the world. Korean electronic goods, such as TV, Refrigerator, Mobile, Computer/Laptop, etc. have become the household name worldwide. The single underlining reason for it is education – the Korean Government meticulously harnessed human resources by introducing appropriate educational system.

It can also be seen how education plays a vital role in economic, political and social development in some of the states in India. Kerala, the state with 100 per cent literacy rate is the most developed state in the country. In Northeast, Mizoram, which has 98 per cent literacy rate, is the fastest growing state in the region. These evidences suggest that undoubtedly, education is the driving force for social, economic and political development of any nation or society.

The importance of education has become all the more crucial today as human society shifts from machine and technology based to 'knowledge based' society. Today, we are living in the age where the maxim 'a nation without knowledge perishes' is absolutely true.[1] It would be extremely difficult for a person, who does not know how to click a computer mouse and send an e-mail to his friends or relatives, in next generations to survive. The Government of India has realized this trend of development and has launched several programmes to bring universal education to every single citizen of the country. The Sarva Shiksa Abhiyan (SSA), which is modified into Right to Education Act (RTEA, 2010) is one of the government's major initiatives to fulfill this vision of providing universal education for the country. Therefore, it is extremely important that every child should be provided with the right kind of education if we desire to bring positive change in the backward region of Northeast hills. However, the ground reality of educational scenario in the northeast hill region, in Manipur in particular, is extremely disheartening.

In this context, a national seminar was organized at Ukhrul by Tangkhul Scholars' Association to deliberate on the pathetic situation of education system in the tribal districts of Manipur. Several papers were presented on various aspects of the topic. This book is the outcome of this seminar, however few other relevant articles have also been added.

In the introductory article of the book, I have tried to discuss the scenario of education in the tribal districts in Manipur. The article looks at the government schools in the villages with critical approach in comparison to private schools. The prevailing conditions of the schools and its consequences, resulting in their abdicating their responsibility to private schools are critically examined. It is my contention that government schools, which are supposed to be the primary provider of education to the poverty stricken tribals of Manipur, have abysmally failed; they have become a liability rather than an asset for the people. This introductory remark of the book intends to initiate a debate as to how to revitalize the government schools in the tribal districts of Manipur and enable them to fulfill their originally intended objective of providing proper education to children. Further, the article intends to invoke a debate whether government schools in the hill area of Manipur are still relevant in view of the prevailing pathetic condition. Should private schools be the better option for the education of the people of the region? If not, what is the alternative?

Formal education in the hills of Manipur was introduced at a late stage, in the last part of 19th century through the Christian Mission. The first school was established at Ukhrul by Rev. William Pettigrew, missionary of Arthington Aborigines Mission. The primary objective of education, then, was to impart the knowledge of reading and writing so that the people would be able to read the Bible and hymn books. Basic mathematics, such as addition, subtraction and multiplication were also taught so as to enable them to do preliminary arithmetic. In the subsequent years, several primary schools and high schools were set up in different hill districts and villages under the initiative of the State Government. In the course of time, education began to be related with employment in the government departments and economic security of the people.

The coming of Roman Catholic Mission in Hill districts of Manipur was a great step in the field of educational development. The Roman Catholic (RC) mission which lays special emphasis on education, established educational institutions wherever they introduced their denomination. One of the schools, which has become popular and the backbone of educational development in Ukhrul district was the Sacred Heart High School at Hundung village. This school has produced several educated second generation leaders as well as bureaucrats, (IAS and IPS officers), academics, social workers and leading politicians among the Tangkhuls. The medium of teaching, which was English, set the trend of English medium schools in the districts of Manipur. People started to consider English as a standard language and those, who could speak English fluently, were graded as of higher status in the social hierarchy. Thus, competition began among the poor parents to send their wards to English medium schools, mostly private schools. Those, who did not want to send their children to the catholic schools due to denominational prejudices, set up their own private schools under the aegis of local church, regional church associations or took individual initiatives for making English the medium of teaching. This trend of setting up private English schools in the hill districts of Manipur set an entirely new paradigm in the history of education in the tribal districts of Manipur. Today, there is a huge demand for English medium private schools in Manipur and private schools managed by churches or individuals are growing like mushroom in every district headquarter and villages.

This new development in education in the hill districts has had both negative and positive impacts on the society. On the positive note, private schools have substituted the defunct government schools and, thus, helped in the process of continuing educational growth in the hill districts of Manipur. Competition among the schools to get more students has, to some extent, improved the quality of education. Students passing out from certain schools are quite good in general and are competitive when they come to college. Moreover, since the medium of teaching is English, the children, who studied in private schools, could communicate in English without much problem. This has resulted in the advantage of getting jobs in private firms like BPOs, Shopping Malls, or restaurants, etc. for young boys and girls, who droped out of schools at secondary and senior secondary levels. Today, there are several boys and girls from Northeast states, who have just secondary level certificates, but are earning for their living in cities like Delhi. Besides, most of the people, who got through competitive exams, like the Union Public Services or State Public Service Commission are from the private school background.

However, there is a serious long term negative consequence of promoting private schools instead of government schools in the larger context. Education has become a commodity, which is bought by paying a high cost. It is obvious that except a few, majority of the parents in the villages do not have regular source of monthly income, but they have to pay their children's school fees on a regular basis. Sending children to private schools has not been a choice, but a compulsion due to unfortunate false notion that children, who study in the government schools, are inferior and rated as being from lower social background. Due to strong prevailing notion that 'government schools are bad' and 'private schools are good', parents do not want to send their wards to government schools.

The practice of family planning has not been popularly accepted in the society due to ignorance or religious belief. This has resulted in each couple having not less than four to five children. Paradoxically, gender equity has improved much and, thus, whether it's a boy or girl, parents ought to send their children to private schools. However, since most of the parents do not have regular income, but depend on the annual income by selling their cash crops like maize or potatoes, they have to rely for their children's monthly school fees on the village money lenders by mortgaging their labour. Parents, who are unable to return the money within a stipulated period, become bonded labour. And hence it perpetuates poverty and aggravates the economic hardship of the people.

But the worst is, due to late payment of schools fees, that children in the school face a lot of embarrassment. Sometimes, they are made to stand in front of their classmates. This has deep psychological effect on the child. The children, who face such situation, develop inferiority complex and become rebellious towards their parents and society at large. During my interaction with many young people, I have come across several young boys, who confessed that they were frustrated due to this problem and discontinued studies and became drug addicts.

In the given situation, it is easy to understand the predicament of the parents. How can a parent, who does not have any regular source of income, give education to their four children by borrowing money till standard ten? Education is a long term investment. It requires a huge investment for a considerable period of time. And the return is very uncertain. The parents, who send their wards to private schools, are not sure about the returns on their investment. But the worst thing is that many children drop out from the schools even before completing education till class twelve, which is the basic required degree for a decent job in the government sector. The point here is, after having invested half of their life time as bonded labour, their children also drop out from the schools and indulge in many undesirable activities that brings mental and psychological stress to them. One can easily understand the plight of the poor parents in the villages due to children's education. This is not just a story, but the reality of our society today.

The false notion that 'government schools are bad and only private schools are good' also affects the morale of the teachers in the government schools. The teachers, who are engaged in government schools, are demoralized and lack seriousness in teaching and other duties. As a result, the government schools in the villages are gradually deteriorating year after year. Today, the so-called government schools in the hill districts are existing only in name without any credible substance. The infrastructure in most of the schools is in a very pathetic condition – school buildings are not better than temporary huts erected in the *jhumming* fields and its difficult to distinguish school compounds from the open fields for animals to roam about, as reflected in the article by Mes Jajo et al.

According to the Educational Profile of Manipur (2011), 'Over one-fifth of the primary schools had no buildings and over two-fifth of the schools were housed in *kutcha* buildings. Sixty per cent of middle schools too were either without buildings or in *kutcha* buildings. Besides, there is complete absence of basic teaching and learning facilities in the schools. In this age of computer, Internet, twitter and facebook, when children are using laptop or Internet instead of books or exercise books or pen in the class room, there are no chairs, tables, benches, and blackboards in the village schools of Manipur hills.

Hence, abdicating the responsibility of education for the children to private schools has had disastrous long term consequences. It has made providing education to children as the biggest burden for the parents in the hill districts of Manipur. If proper study is carried out, I believe, the mess in the government school education in Manipur has negatively impacted the society to the extent of increasing drug addiction, underground activities and extortion and myriad other unhealthy social activities among the youth. This is the reason that I have repeatedly stressed that government schools in hill districts of Manipur are not 'asset but a liability; it has not been a catalyst to transform the society positively, rather it has become a *detrimental factor in taking the society forward'*. The presently existing government schools' education in the hill districts of Manipur has become a den for corruption and moral deprivation for the workers in the schools and agony for the parents. Whether one likes it or not, this is the reality of government school education in the hill districts of Manipur today. Thus, the most serious problem of education system in the hills of Manipur is the non-functioning of the government schools, resulting in the commodification of education by the private entrepreneurs with myriads negative ramifications for the society.

All these are taking place despite huge investment made by the government in the name of 'education for the backward tribals'. According to the Education profile of Manipur (2012), in Ukhrul district alone, there are 158 schools under the Council with six teachers in each school. As per new pay scale, a graduate teacher is paid rupees twenty five thousand and above per month. The total amount of salary for these teachers comes to about rupees two crores, thirty seven lakhs per month or rupees twenty eight crores, forty four lakhs per annum. Besides, there are about 36 high schools having 6-7 teachers in each school. Based on seniority and qualification, a teacher in these schools receive rupees twenty five to thirty thousand as salary in a month. The total amount of money the government invests in these thirty six high schools comes to Rs. 6,048,000 in a month. Apart from this, since 2010, under the RTEA, the government provides free education to every child with uniforms and meals in the school. Inclusive of all these expenses, every month the government spends about seven crore rupees on school education in Ukhrul district alone. Is it not an irony that parents have to mortgage their labour for their children's schools fees, while the government is spending such a huge amount of money on education for their children?

The pertinent questions to be asked here are:

1. Is there any way out from this mess, where the government fund could be put into proper utilization and revive the schools so as to provide better education to our children at lesser cost?
2. Or is it beyond the possible recovery of government schools at this stage and, thus, the only option remaining is private schools? If this is the case, will it not be wiser to abandon government schools once and for all and shift to private schools, so that the fund meant for schools could be diverted to other useful programmes?

In my personal opinion, there is still chance for the government schools to restore their intended purpose and make them productive if there is a will and honest effort among the stakeholders. And this would be the best option for the education of the tribals of Manipur at present. For this, the recruitment system needs to be improved and made free from corruption.

Recruiting the right qualified person to teach children is very crucial for maintaining the basic standard of education in the school. Thus, as a first step, the government must streamline the recruitment system to select qualified teachers for the government schools. In the past, there were no local people, who could teach technical subjects, such as Math, Physics and Chemistry etc. Thus, teachers were brought from the valley, especially the *Meiteis* or *Pangal,* who hardly stayed in the village for one week and took classes for three or four days a week. But today, there are ample qualified local youngsters, who hold B.A., B.Sc. and M.A. and M.Sc. degrees. Many of them are working in BPOs and Shopping Malls and some of them are teaching in private schools. They are willing to teach in the schools, but due to corruption, they are unable to get the government school jobs. If a proper recruitment system, free from corruption and political interference is introduced, these bright youngsters could be recruited for teaching our children in the schools. This will bring a new revolution in the government schools in the villages.

Therefore, proper recruitment system should be introduced where no politician or influential people could ever interfere in the recruiting process. The best option would be to outsource the recruitment of teachers to an agency outside the state. Secondly, no interview is required since it has become a means of corruption; thus, written examination should be made the final criteria for the selection of teachers.

Apart from this, education in our society should strive to promote entrepreneurship by imparting the spirit of creativity in our children's mind. As Ringkahao's articles pointed out, the school syllabus of Manipur Board of Education needs to be re-examined. Nature has provided abundant resources to us. Education system should be such that it equips students with the skill to appropriate resources form nature and use it for the progress and development of the society. Therefore, the content of our school syllabus should be to instill a sense of inquiry and creativity in the minds of young people. Education system should aim to produce innovators and wealth creators out of the natural resources available in our land.

Is education in our society meeting this objective? Honestly, the present education system in our society is far from what is desired. Unfortunately, we just imitate what is being imposed on us from outside without much thinking. This kind of education provides only the knowledge to read, to write and arithmetic for getting employment. Such a system of education makes us dependent rather than independent. The result is that after receiving degrees/certificates, one has to go begging for jobs to the ministers or those who are in authority. In light of this, we need to re-examine the content and syllabus of our education system and bring necessary changes, so that education would make our children innovative and enterprising.

Knowledge comes from communication and communication requires language. Without proper means of communication or language, knowledge cannot develop. The presence of Japanese, Chinese and Koreans in every field today has been possible because they can read and write through their own languages. This has given them a lot of advantages for progress and development in many fields. English is good to learn, but it cannot really be a tool of education and development, especially for the rural masses. It is necessary to make an effort to have our own literature, so that books are written in the language that everyone can read and enrich their knowledge.

The book 'Rethinking Education in the Hills of Northeast India' consists of twelve articles. Most of the articles were presented in the seminar conducted by Tangkhul Scholars Association (TSA) at Ukhrul in 2012. There are also articles, which were not presented and their themes may not be directly in line with the theme of the book. However, the articles are concerned with the issues pertaining to the tribals of Manipur. Because of this, some of the articles have been included. Some of the articles are not purely academic in strict sense of the term; but most of these are concerned with the practical problems of education in the present context. Therefore, the book will be useful for the academics, social activists, civil society leaders and mostly for policy makers in the field of education, particularly for the tribals in Manipur. The contributors are mostly academics, who have done research in different fields in the region of Northeast India.

'Pettigrew's Children: History of Print Culture of Tangkhul Language' article by Dr. A.S. Shimreiwung traces the origin of print culture in the tribal literature of Manipur, particularly the Tangkhuls. The print culture in tribal literature was first introduced by Rev. William Pettigrew, when he established a primary school at Ukhrul in 1896. Since then, several indigenous writers have arisen from among the Tangkhuls. Despite shortcomings, these writers have paved the way for further development of print culture of literature in the tribal society of Manipur in general and Tangkhuls in particular.

Mr A.C. Kharingpam's article 'Colonial Ideology and the Early 20th Century Text: An Overview of Hegemony in the School Texts of Manipur' analyses how the education in Manipur is being used as a channel to promote state ideology and thus, education system was being reduced to a mere instrument in the hand of the state for its survival. Several myths and poetic narration in the school curriculum of the education in Manipur is the clear evidence of this fact.

Article on 'Bankruptcy of Education: Ideology and Literature in the Context of Tangkhul Society' by Mr. Yuimirin Kapai is a critical analysis of the Tangkhul writers. He examines the ideological underpinning of the education system, which is embedded in the social structure. With the theoretical framework so established, he tries to look into the phenomenal paucity of artists among the Tangkhuls and the pervasive philistinism.

'Traditional Knowledge, Social-Cultural Practices and Modern Education' article by Dr. Tuisem Ngakang, discusses the social transformation, which came with the introduction of modern education and new western religion. Tuisem argues that the coming of modern religion, Christianity, which brought formal education in the tribal society, has resulted in the disappearance of many traditional social and cultural practices. This has, in one sense, resulted in uprooting Tangkhul society from its tradition and culture.

In article 'Curricula and Education System of Manipur State', Dr. Ringkahoa Horam makes observations on the existing education system of Manipur, particularly the syllabus for schools. He argues that if education is a journey of life, then the syllabus for the student is the road map of the journey. A carefully planned and clearly written comprehensive syllabus is one of the most important resources we need to provide to the students. In this regard, the syllabus and the education system in Manipur is far behind to meet the required standard.

Article 'Tangkhul-Naga Grammar: A Study of Word Formation' by Dr. Victor Ahum, brings out a proper grammatical form of Tangkhul langauge. It is an innovative analysis of how to put tribal language in a correctly understandable form of dialect.

In article, 'Social Enquiry of Educational Scenario: The Mapithel (Pesii) Range of Ukhrul District, Manipur', Dr. Mes Jajo, Ms. Lucy Jajo and Mr. Maheishang Awungshi bring out the reality of the existing government schools in one of the tribal areas of Ukhrul district. The authors clearly bring out and prove that all the criticism of the government schools in Manipur were not wrong. The extremely pathetic situation of the government schools in the hill districts of Manipur are a reality rather than just a prejudicial assumption by the critics of the government.

'Education and Spirituality in the Present Context' article by Dr. R. Wonkhuimi is about the necessity of spiritual education. She views that imparting spiritual education would make education a wholesome venture and make educated person really humane, who would care for the society.

Ms. Lucy Jajo Shimray's article on 'Women Education and its Potential of Harnessing Sustainable Handloom Industry in Northeast' harnesses the resource of the traditional skill inherited by the women folk of tribals in Manipur for their economically sustainable livelihood. The author explores the potential possessed by the womanhood of Northeast tribals.

'Right to Education (RTE) Act 2009: Its Relevance in Manipur written by Mr. Thothuingam Shinglai critically analyses how the new education right called the Right to Education is relevant and effectively possible to implement in the tribal districts of Manipur.

Article 'Education and Identity Formation: Some Reflections on the History of the Nagas of Chandel District (with Special Reference to the Monsang Nagas)' by Mr. W. Somie Monsang is an analysis of the role of education in evolving the Monsang identity. According to him, the identity of Monsang is being gradually evolved through various stages of crisis and distortion by colonial writers. However, it was the introduction of western education, which played a crucial role in clarifying all those misinterpretations and brought Monsang as a tribe at the present stage.

'Traditional Forest Management through Indigenous Knowledge

and Practices in Northeast India: A Case Study in Tangkhul Community, Manipur' article by Mr. Franky Varah and Mr. T. Shimrah focuses on the impact of modern education introduced by the Christian missionaries on the socio-cultural aspects of the Nagas. The influence of Christian missionaries is manifested in every aspect of Naga life. Thus, there are good reasons to begin with missionary activities in the case of the colonization of the Nagas. Franky argues that Christian missionaries represent the most intrusive and transformative agent to bring a change in the Tangkhul society. In pursuing this sustained policy of change, the missionaries have demonstrated a more radical commitment to rule than political administrators did.

Notes and References

Here, I used the term 'knowledge' in tandem with education. It is so because knowledge comes from imparting proper education to people, though not all the information getting through educational institutions are necessarily knowledge, in a sense.

Michael J. and Seth James. (2011). 'Popular Demand and Education in South Korea: An Historical Overview'. Madison University: USA.

Kim, Do young. (2012). 'Christianity, Education and Economic Development in Korea', Seminar paper presented at Ukhrul.

Educational profile of Manipur, (2012) www.E-pao.net

Patil, R., (2012). Role of Education in Social Change, *International Educational E-Journal*, {Quarterly}, Volume-I, Issue-II, Jan-Feb-Mar 2012).

Parankimali, J. (2012). Meaning, Nature and Aims of Education, Johnpara kimalil.wordpress.com

2

Pettigrew's Children

History of Print Culture of Tangkhul Language

A.S. Shimreiwung

The author traces the trajectories in print culture of Tangkhul language from its nascent stage to contemporary time. The adoption of written culture by Tangkhuls, who were practising oral culture during the pre-colonial period, has come to be seen as one of the success stories of White missionary's work among the tribes of Northeast India. Because of the lack of proper historical sources on print literature of Tangkhul Nagas; it has become extremely difficult to trace the history of publications that has taken place in Tangkhul language. The unavailability of most of the printed literary works has handicapped researchers in this field. Nevertheless, the mission reports submitted by Christian missionaries and local history written by native authors have feliciatated in mapping the history of print culture of Tangkhul language.

The appropriation of print culture by Tangkhuls indicates the cultural process, generally experienced by almost all the tribes in Northeast India, by which a new medium, which literacy theorist called the 'technology of writing', for communication and creative expressions have come to dominate the traditional medium. According to Jack Goody, the interface between oral and written culture takes place in three different modes:

(a) 'meeting of cultures with and without writing',
(b) interface of written and oral culture in societies that employ writing to varying degrees, and

(c) 'the use of writing and speech in the linguistic life of an individual'.[1]

In the historical and cultural context of Tangkhuls, we may draw the analogy that the appropriation of print culture by the Tangkhuls from White missionaries was a case of meeting between two different cultures. Print culture was absent among the Tangkhuls, and it began only after the advent of Colonialism and Christian missionaries in their society. However, in understanding the historical context and cultural process through which Tangkhuls have adopted print culture, we also need to keep in mind that 'written culture' has no cultural primacy over oral culture, and with the adoption of written culture, the oral tradition has not lost its relevance. Walter J. Ong has also argued that writing did not reduce orality, but enhanced it by making it "possible to organize the 'principles' or constituents of oratory into scientific 'art'."[2] Therefore, instead of assuming that print culture reduced the significance of oral culture, we need to see the extension of traditional arts and the adoption of new technology in the field of communication and art. Even after the adoption of print culture, the practice and relevance of oral culture remains in literate societies. The history and impact of print culture in Tangkhul society can also be analyzed in the aspects of complimentary relations between different modes of cultural practices in society, rather than assuming that print culture and oral culture are poles apart or destroy the significance of one medium or the other.

Beginning of Print Culture in Tangkhul Language: Rev. William Pettigrew's Literary Works among the Tangkhul Nagas

Rev. William Pettigrew's *Tangkhul Naga Grammar and Dictionary* written in 1918 remains to this day as one of the most authoritative book on Tangkhul language and it is still relied by almost all the literate Tangkhuls. This book primarily consists of detailed deliberation on Tangkhul language, which was written in English, and also contains the dictionary of Tangkhul words translated into English. And, it was the first book that highlighted the grammatical rules of Tangkhul language. Although, recent research on Tangkhul language has highlighted certain flaws in Pettigrew's formulation of

Tangkhul language, there has been no major published work on Tangkhul language. However, if we look deeper into the contribution of Rev. W. Pettigrew to Tangkhul language, it exceeds far beyond the reduction of oral language into written culture. One of the distinctive characteristic of Tangkhuls has been linguistic diversity, where every village has its own dialect. Although, the neighboring villages could comprehend each other's dialect, people from far flung villages could not understand each other. In such a situation, choosing a particular dialect as the common language for the entire tribes must have been a difficult task. In the *Preface* to *Tangkhul Naga Grammar and Dictionary,* Rev. W. Pettigrew also mentioned that:

> "In this tribe [Tangkhuls], it can be truly said that almost every village… has its separate dialect. Ukhrul, the most important and influential village of the tribe, having been decided upon, in 1896 as the headquarters of the Mission, its dialect has been reduced to writing, and this Grammar only professes to be an investigation of that dialect. The policy of bringing in from the surrounding villages suitable students to the Training school at Ukhrul leads the way to a gradual unification of the language."[3]

Given the linguistic diversity of the Tangkhuls, unification of all the Tangkhul village dialects is an insurmountable task, even from today's situation. However, his idea of forming a 'common language' for all the Tangkhul villages, and using the school as the tool to achieve that goal has been an ingenious method. One may also interpret Rev. William Pettigrew's decision to choose Ukhrul dialect for transliteration into written script as guided by convenience, since the first Mission school and centre was decided upon to be set in Ukhrul.

While describing about the method employed in the transliteration of Tangkhul language, Pettigrew wrote that:

> "Twenty years ago, when reducing this [Tangkhul] language to writing, I used the Roman characters, and followed Hunterian method of transliteration. Whatever school books and portions of Scriptures we have, have been prepared on the above method."[4]

Before the publication of *Tangkhul Grammar and Dictionary,* Rev. W. Pettigrew had done massive printing and translation works, not only in Tangkhul language, but also with the languages of other communities, like Manipuri. This book, which was written with assistance from Assam Government, seems to be a culmination of all the linguistic works that Rev. Pettigrew had been doing for Tangkhul language. In this book, he has also analyzed the close resemblance between Tangkhul language and Manipuri, or considered it as one of the cognates of Manipuri.[5] However, in a review of this book, T.C. Hodson wrote that:

> "A sketch of Tangkhul Naga grammar appeared in vol. iii, pt. ii, of the Linguistic Survey of India, when it was assigned to the Naga Kuki group of the Tibeto-Burman family of Indo-Chinese languages. The classification of these languages in accordance with the sound philology and phonetic principles is a task of considerable magnitude… The author's intimate knowledge of Meithei has enabled him to point to many parallels and similarities. Tangkhul, however, differs from Meithei in its numeric systems and the method of forming the negative, both important characteristics."[6]

Rev. W. Pettigrew's intimate knowledge of Meithei and earlier association with it, as T.C. Hodson has remarked, seem to have determined his interest in drawing the similarities between Tangkhul and Meitei languages. However, later researchers on Tangkhul language have classified it as a distinct linguistic sub-family, 'Luhupa' in the pantheon of tribal languages in NortheastIndia.[7] He did identify the nuances of Tangkhul language as primarily depended on phonetic principles. The significance of sound in relation to meanings of the words and not strictly on syllables still remain as one of the major issues in Tangkhul language.

When he took up the mission work in Manipur in 1896, Tangkhul was one of the first tribal languages that he had tried to reduce to writing and printing. He had certain options pertaining to the use of script for Tangkhul language, as he had already learnt Bengali and Manipuri; however, he preferred to use Roman characters for the school in Ukhrul. In one of the mission reports, Rev. W. Pettigrew explains the predicament that he faced while choosing the script for Tangkhul language.

"For the school at Ukhrul, it was decided to introduce the Roman character. At first the boys started with a small English primer, and after the primer in their own language was prepared and printed, they started on this as well, so that they [could] learn to read and write their own tongue as well as English. Bengali would be of little use to them, so it has been discarded, although it might be worthwhile later on to teach them the character, for the purpose of reading Manipuri, a language they are familiar with."[8]

While carrying out the translation of Gospels into Tangkhul, transliterating Tangkhul language, and preparing school textbooks for school in Ukhrul, Rev. Pettigrew preferred English and Tangkhul languages for Tangkhul students in Ukhrul over other forms of language. The significance of native language as the mode for reading and writing for Tangkhuls had been recognized by Rev. William Pettigrew from the very beginning when Tangkhul primers were prepared for the schools. The adoption of native language over other languages of the neighbouring communities has turned out to be a visionary step towards the development of print culture in Tangkhul language. It has also helped the Tangkhuls to write and engage in literary creativity in their own native language, which has significant impact on the identity formation of the tribe.

Tangkhul language is highly tonal and the usage of Roman characters has proved to be a daunting task, both for the writers as well as the readers in this language. By adding two letters, *ā* and *a*, to the existing letters of Roman characters, Rev. W. Pettigrew was able to employ Roman characters for Tangkhul language and prepare the written text in Tangkhul. However, even at present, capturing the tonal characters of Tangkhul language by employing the letters and sound of Roman characters remains a problematic issue.

The initial years of Rev. and Mrs. Pettigrew's mission work in Ukhrul were devoted to producing textbooks for schools and publication of Gospels in Tangkhul. Thus, the beginning of print culture in Tangkhul language primarily consists of small textbooks and some translated Gospels. When the Mission School in Ukhrul was established in 1897, there was no Tangkhul textbook to be used for students; therefore, an English textbook called '*Step by Step*' was used as a textbook for the students.[9] After meticulous effort to understand Tangkhul language, Rev. William Pettigrew prepared the First and Second Primers as textbooks for the Mission School in Ukhrul during 1897 and 1898.[10] Even after hundred years of its publication, his book *Tangkhul Primer* is still in use as Tangkhul textbook for primary students in schools.

He also mentioned that help from his elder students in school had been utilized while preparing the first Biblical publication of the Tangkhuls. The *Gospel of Luke* from *The Holy Bible* was the first translated Biblical text to be printed in Tangkhul language in 1902.[11] It is not sure which version of Bible they had employed while translating the scriptures, as such information has not been given, and the printed version of the translated book remains unavailable.

The First and Second Primers in Tangkhul, which Rev. Pettigrew had prepared, were mainly for foundational course for reading and writing in Tangkhul. He, however, mentioned that the Third and Fourth Primer in Tangkhul consist of *Life of Jesus Christ.* While he seemed to be busy in Ukhrul, concentrating mainly on the translation and school work, the printing of these books were done in Calcutta. He had sent series of manuscripts from Ukhrul and also took the consultation of other scholars for his published works, while he kept on producing one book after another.

The first proper hymn book in Tangkhul, *Jesuwui Lā: Hymns in Tāngkhul Nāga,* was published in 1907.[12] Although the main author of this hymn book was Rev. William Pettigrew, he acknowledged the help of his students while preparing this hymnbook.[13] The hymn book contains 51 translated songs, with proper lyrical verses.[14] However, musical notations were not included with the songs in the first two editions, except the tonal keys. In the third edition of *Jesuwui Laa Lairik* in 1929, which was printed in London, for the first time, musical notation Tonic Solfa was included with the hymns in Tangkhul. Going through the text of the hymns, one could find the base for mode of lyrical composition in Tangkhul language was laid down by this hymnbook. Although, there are numerous flaws in words and letters in this hymnbook, there are similarities as well between the present Tangkhul hymnbooks and hymns in *Jesuwui Lā,* which is in terms of lyrical style and some words. The mode of composing songs in lyric or poetic form was not totally new to the Tangkhuls, folksongs are an oral mode of lyrical poetry. However, we can notice the introduction of new modes of song-writing in this hymnbook, which is more attuned to Western poetry and lyrics.

The school textbooks, which were prepared by Rev. Pettigrew and his students in Ukhrul School, had tremendously contributed to the formation of Tangkhul language and literature. The first students of Rev. W. Pettigrew's Mission School in Ukhrul were not only instrumental in the transliteration of Tangkhul language, but also pioneers in various modes of writing. The Tangkhul students of Rev. W. Pettigrew, who took up the task of writing were: M.K. Shimray, R.K. Luikham, and S. Kanrei.[15] The contribution of Rev. W. Pettigrew to Tangkhul language, in terms of books and Biblical texts and hymns, are enormous, even in today's standard. He had published numerous books in Tangkhul, inclusive school textbooks, hymnals, Bibles, and dictionary, during his 40 years of mission work in Manipur. The titles of his books in Tangkhul, according to Rev C. Kaping, are:

(1) *Tangkhul Primer* (*First and Second*),
(2) *Tanglen Lairik,*
(3) *Otshan Lairik,*
(4) *Kuipang Lairik,*
(5) *Kazat Makharanuda Sakhangachon Lairik (Part 1 and 2),*
(6) *Jesu Khararchan (Part 1 and 2),*
(7) *Matthew* (Gospel),
(8) *Mark* (Gospel),
(9) *Luke (*Gospel),
(10) *John* (Gospel),
(11) *Jesuwui La Lairik,*
(12) *New Testament, Tangkhul Naga.*[16]

The publication of the whole set of *New Testament* in Tangkhul in 1926 appears to be the last publication of Rev. W. Pettigrew in Tangkhul language.[17] Although, he failed to publish the full set of *The Holy Bible,* the task of Bible translation in Tangkhul was initiated and the need of Tangkhul Christians was met in certain aspects. And, as many *Gospels* from the *New Testament* were already published, it was just a matter of time that the full set would appear. Going by the title of books published by him, the *New Testament* in Tangkhul may be considered as a major translation work that had been done by him.

In all these translation and printing works that Rev. W. Pettigrew had taken up in Tangkhul language, his concern seems to have been directed by two major aims: educational and religious purposes. He did succeed in not only giving the Tangkhuls the scripts for writing, but also made them learn how to read and write in their own language and English. Moreover, the spread of Christianity in Tangkhul was also aided by the use of written culture. The area, which he seems to have neglected was secular writings. Unlike the colonial officers, Rev. W. Pettigrew has not produced any monographs, except some articles about Tangkhul's ritual of the death, *Kathi Kasam.* And, we didn't find any of his writings in Tangkhul that deals with serious literary works, like poetry and essays.

The Emergence of Native Writers

Among the students of Rev. W. Pettigrew, Miksha K. Shimray was one of the first Tangkhul to take up writing and translation work. M.K. Shimray wrote two books for the first time, which were *Jesuwui Khararchan* (in prose) and *Yurka Eina Kata Lairik* (Poetry), primarily as textbooks for school.[18] Given the fact that Tangkhuls were following oral culture before the arrival of White Missionaries; the literary acts of writing poetry and prose in Tangkhul language, through written narratives, were a new form of creativity. Although the act of writing and publishing works among the early native writers were largely motivated by the need to have school textbooks for higher classes, the native writers were introducing new forms of literary art in Tangkhul language, which the later generation would rely on. M.K. Shimray was also one of the first native writers, who wrote scores of books in English. Some of the books, which M.K, Shimray had written are:

1. *Notes on Bible Reading* (1935),
2. *Lesson Preparations and Teaching Method* (1956),
3. *Church History* (1957),
4. *Harmony of the Gospel* (1960),

5. *James (Notes)* (1956),
6. *Hebrews (Notes)* (1956),
7. *The Coming of Christ* (1958).[19]

Not much is known about the contents of these books as these are no longer available. It cannot be ascertained whether the books he has written were all in English or in Tangkhul language, however, according to C. Chiphang, he had the flair to write both in English and Tangkhul. The titles of these books suggest that most of the writings of M.K. Shimray were concerned with Biblical text and manual for Pastors and Sunday Schools. The last major publication of M.K. Shimray was *Tangkhul Miwurlung,* which was published in 1967.[20] Unfortunately, this book also remains unavailable now. However, some reference to this book indicates that it deals with the history and traditional culture of Tangkhul Nagas. Later on, this book was also used as textbook for high school students in Tangkhul. As noted by C. Chiphang, Y.K. Shimray's contribution to the field of Tangkhul literature and written language has been quite distinctive in various aspects.[21]

Other native writers, who took up writing were R.K. Luikham and S. Kanrei. The Tangkhul Literature Society's historical records shows that R.K. Luikham had written *Chishutmi,* a school textbook for Class V.[22] *Chishutmi* was divided into two parts, *Akhum I* (book 1) and *Akhum II* (book 2), and it was first published in 1957.[23] The contents of *Chishutmi: Akhum II* indicates that it is collection of essays, poetries, short stories from *The Holy Bible* and Tangkhul folk tales. The diversity of subjects and themes in this small textbook, which consists of 67 pages and 18 chapters, is astounding. One can discern certain distinctive aspects in the art of writing, which the native writers had employed and the issues that they had emphasized through the nature and contents of the textbooks. Two chapters in *Chishutmi: Akhum II* were transliteration of Tangkhul folktales, another two chapters were stories from *The Holy Bible,* one chapter on Greek Mythology (Leonidas), one chapter on modern personality (Florence Nightingale), and the rest of essay chapters are mainly concerned with Christian values, such as *Nava-Navali Khayaklu* (Be Respectful to Parents) and *Morei Kaphara* (The Birth of Sin). Most of the poetries were also concerned with hardship in life and moral values. The early school textbooks serve as the platform for native writers to initiate new form of literary works, which were massive departure from oral literature in their style of presentation and contents. The students, who studied the textbooks written by early native writers, were in turn influenced by their style of writing and usages. If we make a comparison between the oral literature, like folktales and folksongs, with modern forms of writing like prose and poetry in school textbooks, there are numerous distinctions to be noted. One major aspects of new form literary work is that these are massively influenced by English literary form, which the native writers have learnt as a part of their schooling.

R. Luikham's *Wung Tangkhul Mayonza,* which was published in 1961, and M.K. Shimray's *Tangkhul Miwurlung* (1967), can be considered as the advent of proper form of book writing and publication by native authors. These books served as a departure from earlier attention of native writers that was driven by the forms of textbook writing and publication, which primarily consisted of short stories and poetry. The publication of a proper book, which deals with broad theme and intensive deliberation on a given subject, began to emerge with the publication of R. Luikham and M.K. Shimray's works. These books also signify a new shift from orientation towards biblical text and discourse, to which the missionaries and early native writers had initially given much attention. These books deal primarily with the factual accounts of the Tangkhuls, their history, culture and traditions, which were in oral forms during those periods. Therefore, the value of these books does not lie in their contribution to literature, but more on the ethnographic and historical accounts of the Tangkhul, which were written from natives' perspective.

Tangkhul Literature Society and Indigenous Text Book Publication

After the textbook publication that had been initiated by Rev. W. Pettigrew, the task of writing textbook for schools were taken up by Tangkhul writers, who had been educated in Mission schools. There was a massive proliferation of schools during the first half of 20th century among the Tangkhuls, with the progress of Christianization. Wherever Christianity found foothold in a village, the new institutions that were ultimately established were: Mission schools and Church.

Among those mission school educated Tangkhuls, some of them felt the desired need to form an organization that would take up the task of developing Tangkhul language. In 1938, Ng. Ragui called a meeting to discuss about the formation of Tangkhul literary society. Twelve individuals came to take part in the deliberation for Tangkhul language, where the members present unanimously took the decision to establish the 'Tangkhul Literature Society' (TLS).[24] The members of TLS took the initiative by writing articles and taking up the compilation of Tangkhul textbooks for the enhancement of Tangkhul language. Though literate Tangkhuls had already contributed towards school textbooks, the concerted effort by a society and group of individuals for the development of Tangkhul language was absent before the formation of TLS. The formation of TLS and its literary activities are significant for Tangkhul language in various aspects. First of all, it heralds the overall control over Tangkhul textbooks by a specific organization devoted to the development of Tangkhul language. Secondly, with the formation of TLS, the task of textbook writing and linguistic development of Tangkhul was taken up by non-religious organization and individuals.

After six-seven years of TLS existence, numerous articles in Tangkhul language had been collected; however, before publishing these articles in the form of a textbook, TLS decided to circulate it in the form of a 'Magazine'.[25] Thus, the TLS magazine *Zingthanwo* was published under the editorship of Y.K. Shimray. *Zingthanwo* was the first magazine/journal to be published in Tangkhul and a new form of publication work, as there was no newspaper or magazine in those days. The history of TLS has recorded that their activities were hampered by 'Japanese war[26]' during 1944. Most of their printed documents and the magazine *Zingthanwo* were burnt down along with their houses during the war. The attempt to revive *Zingthanwo* after the war was also met with failure due to financial problems.

TLS has contributed towards the enhancement of Tangkhul language in numerous ways. After the end of the colonial era, most of the activities of TLS began to bear fruit. The Government of Manipur had not allowed Tangkhul language, including other tribal languages to be taught in schools. In 1975, TLS succeeded in pressurizing the Manipur Government to approve Tangkhul language to be taught in schools in Manipur.[27] Further in 1977, they also got the order from Manipur Government to make Tangkhul language the medium of instructions in Ukhrul. During these periods, Tangkhul language was only taught in primary and lower classes, however, in 1985, TLS also got the approval to introduce Tangkhul language text *Meiwon* for Class IX and X.[28]

Apart from the effort to get official recognition of Tangkhul language for teaching as a subject in schools, TLS also engaged in the development of Tangkhul language by taking up the transliteration of folk tales, review the grammatical usage and spellings errors in Tangkhul language. Currently, most of their activities have remained within the domain of school textbooks and Tangkhul language. On the flipside, the activities of TLS have not been able to move into serious literary works and publications. Though the nomenclature of TLS implies 'literature' as the major area of emphasis, it has remained and functions as a 'linguistic' society. Constraints on the part of TLS is largely related to the problems of Tangkhul language and the attempt to create standardization has also not succeeded so far.

Major Literary Works in Tangkhul Language: Novellas and Poetry

Most of the senior members of TLS classified genres of literary work into two parts: prose/essays and poetry. Given the practice that early Tangkhul textbooks used and still continue to do, textbooks were classified into two as prose and poetry sections. It is a general understanding that these two distinct forms of literary works prevail among the early Tangkhul writers. However, the art of literary writing that were introduced and imbibed through the school textbooks has influenced Tangkhul literature to a large extent. Though print culture was a new medium, which was appropriated from other culture, the hold of traditional arts over new forms of literary works were seen in most of the early Tangkhul literature. These aspects can be seen in the massive transliteration of Tangkhul folktales by TLS for school textbooks and in the works of K.K. Hugh. Y.K. Shimray, P.R. Yangkahao and others, who can be considered as later generation of native writers. Although the themes in their literary work were largely based on Tangkhul folk-traditions, their style of written narratives was highly influenced by English literature. Thus, in the initial period, Tangkhul literary works were characterized by amalgamation of folk and modern themes. These forms of literary works can be seen in the works of Y.K. Shimray's *Tangkhul Poetry: Book I*, which was reprinted in 1977-78, so probably published early. There are seven poetries in *Tangkhul Poetry,* which include themes like: *Maitonphy, Mara Eina Thngajanwon, Lungleng Philava, Chamtha Eina Chamthay, Timrawon, Sampheirok,* and *Tangkhul Ngalei.*[29] Except the last poetry *Tangkhul Ngalei*, which has become the theme song of Tangkhuls and is even included in Tangkhul hymnal *Khokharum Laa,* all other poetries are based on Tangkhul folktales. In the pantheon of Tangkhul literary works, these poetries by Y.K. Shimray have remained as the most significant attempt to integrate two forms of literary genre: oral folktales and modern poetry. Let us consider the text from his poetry *Maitonphy.*

> *"Khuiphalungra, Maitonlali,*
> *Tahangmilu, thakta taolu,*
> *Kathi phamei okathuili,*
> *Haplui, haplui machialu,*
> *Mazamara naniwui zat,*
> *Mamangmara naniwui khor,*
> *Khuirafalu iwui khavat,*
> *Akhuimilu iwui kahor.*"[30]

With these dramatic imageries and dialogue, Y.K. Shimray began the poetic narrative in the adaptation from the popular Tangkhul folktale of Maitonphy and Shimreishang. The narrative above not only captures the angst in the protagonist Shimreishang, but also introduces a new form of narration of Tangkhul folktales. The narratives style adopted in this poetry also seems well suited for 'drama writing'. What we can ascertain from the text above is a simple adaptation of rhyming and rhythm of English poetry, yet beautifully crafted. Apart from Y.K. Shimray, we have not come across many Tangkhul writers using similar style of writing, with equal respect for the local idioms and poetic rules. Although there have been numerous attempts by Tangkhul writers to write poetry in proper form, such standards have not been maintained so far.

Another notable poet in Tangkhul literature is R. Suisa, whose literary works remain to be taught in schools. He has introduced a new form of poetry writing in Tangkhul, which unfortunately, has not been followed by other writers. His poetry *Huinakhar* is exceptional in certain aspects of poetry writing in Tangkhul literature.[31]

> "Mha, mayansānpai mamalaipai
> Mha, khāngshok khāngzang, khanta, khāngkā,
> Kathem thangkhamei ngachei ngarok;
> Matungshin majirar akhamang,
> Khanao khari khayei khayeipai.
> Kateo kahak pam ongarokpai.
> Kathai katho sheung sheivāpai.
> Okathui ngatak, harva khongpei.
> Āya aj na akhama shok,
> Āya yangda āja karsangra.
> Shokkahai rākahai kachishut,
> Tākakam shokluira raluira.
> Ākhama āj yangvāra,
> Ārui ngayung, ānaolam āton;
> Thangthang ngaironron shokrāsāra,
> Shokthanghon theikhuira huinakhār."[32]

The beauty of these verses by R. Suisa lies in exploring the linguistic quality of Tangkhul linguistic idioms. By emphasizing more on the rhythmic value in the poetic narratives, the poetry-writing takes a new aspect where Tangkhul words can be synchronously formed by following the tones of every word. The usage of the root words like '*Khakhang*' (to lift) into '*khangshok, khangzang, khangta, khangzang*' are generally found only in Suisa's writing. The tonal aspects in poetry writing, which Suisa's poetry has indicated, are something that need to be explored further.

The art of poetry writing adopted by later writers, like M.C. Arang's *Tangkhul Laasem,* has not followed the pattern of R. Suisa or Y.K. Shimray's style of poetry writing. And, unfortunately, most of the Tangkhul poetries have not been able to maintain the literary quality as well as themes. If one compares Tangkhul poetry with the song lyrics of *Akui,* we will find that the literary art has not been fully explored, as lyrical text has more quality in terms of usage of words and emotions. Overall, some of the major impediments in the growth of Tangkhul are that there have been no major publication of Tangkhul poetry in recent times and not many writers are seriously engaged in poetry writing in recent times.

The emergence of novel in Tangkhul language can be considered as a major literary change, as it varies from folk-narratives to a great extent. Kongsui Luithui's *Machapalu Leikashiva* has been considered as the first novel published in Tangkhul language.[33] The novel as a form of literary narrative is contemporaneous, and its subject deals with life experiences that are closer to real life situations than other forms of writing. There have been numerous novel writers in Tangkhul language and the publication of short novellas continues unabated. Considering the length and plots in Tangkhul novels, most of the so called 'Tangkhul novels' would fall into the category of novellas. Most of the novels are published by the individual authors and private circulation is still the norm followed by most authors. Among the novels in Tangkhul language, Khamshim A. Shimray's *Shairengwon, Khiapawu Khayon Khala,* and *Thumkahai Leishat* can be considered as important novels. The theme and plots in most of Khamshim's novels represent the contrast and conflict between modern life and traditional values and customs. One can compare such form of literary works with the African post-colonial literature, like Chinua Achebe's *Things Fall Apart*. Women authors writing Tangkhul novels are still rare; like hunting, writing seems to have become a man's work. Leimiwon has remained the only woman novelist in Tangkhul literature. She has written numerous novels on her own. Her initial works, like *Maranao wui Mirin* lacks the literary standard, and it is replete with grammatical errors. However, in her later novel, like *Tangkhul Avaram* and *Iram Wonra,* she has improved the narrative styles and plots to a great extent. In some aspects, she has contributed to Tangkhul literature by bringing in the views from women's aspect to contemporary situations. Her novels are generally centered on the theme of 'overcoming the tragedy' that one faces in life. In an interview in Ukhrul, she told me that writing gives the strength to face the tragedy that she has personally faced. She also mentioned that all she earns is spent on book publication; however, she finds satisfaction in what she does; through writing novels and publication work, she feels that she is contributing to the advancement of Tangkhul society.

In the genre of translation work, Stephen Angkang's *Genevieve* still remains as one of the major literary works. Apart from biblical translations and hymnals, not much translation of literature of other languages into Tangkhul has been taken up by Tangkhul writers. The varieties of literary genre in Tangkhul novella has also been limited to a large extent. New forms of writing like autobiography and biography of certain prominent individuals, like *Ruichumhao, R. Suisa* has also been taken up. And, there is no publication in the field of drama writing in Tangkhul literature. Therefore, in the field of literature, Tangkhul writers and authors have much work to accomplish.

Conclusion

The history of print culture in Tangkhul language indicates that Tangkhuls have been able to appropriate the art and skill of writing to the full extent. Publication works have proliferated into various areas and localities. However, serious literature in Tangkhul language has not been taken up by many authors and writers. The publication works as well as literary writing in Tangkhul language have remained to be textbook centric. Most of the Tangkhul writers have written only to contribute to the school textbooks. TLS and Christian Literature Society have been the only publication houses that have been consistently publishing books in Tangkhul. The art and technology of writing and producing literary works may be considered as constituting different levels of linguistic activity. However, cursory observation indicates that Tangkhul language has not advanced much in the field of literature, although the literacy rate in Ukhrul is as high as the national average.

References

1. Goody, Jack. 1987. *The Interface between the Written and the Oral,* Cambridge University Press, p. ix.
2. Ong, Walter J. 1982. *Orality and Literacy: The Technologizing of the Word,* Taylor and Francis, p. 9.
3. Pettigrew, Rev. W. 1918. *Tangkhul Naga Grammar and Dictionary,* Ukhrul: Manipur (Reprinted by Tangkhul Naga Baptist Convention, 1979).

4. *Ibid.*, p. 1.
5. *Ibid.*, p. 2.
6. Hodson, T.C. 1919. Review (Untitled), *Journal of the Royal Asiatic Society of Great Britain and Ireland*, (Apr., 1919), pp. 249-253.
7. Matisoff, James A. 1972. "Tangkhul Naga and Comparative Tibeto-Burman", *Tonan Ajia Kenkyu (The South East Asian Studies)* Vol. 10, No. 2, September 1972.
8. *The Baptist Missionary Magazine,* Vol. LXXVIII, 1898.
9. Shimray, Y.K. and Z. Maransa. 1993. *Tangkhul Literature Society Rinchan* (in Tangkhul), UKhrul: Published by Tangkhul Literature Society, p. 1.
10. Pettigrew, Rev. William. 1899. 'Report from the Tangkhul Naga Field', *The Assam Mission of ABMU,* 1899.
11. *The Baptist Missionary Magazine,* Vol. LXXVII, 1902.
12. Pettigrew, Rev. W.
13. *Ibid.*
14. Pettigrew, Rev. W. 1907. *Jesuwui Lā: Hymns in Tāngkhul Nāga* (in Tangkhul), Assam: Published by American Baptist Mission House, Ukhrul, Manipur.
15. Chiphang, C. 2006. "Tangkhul Wordham Otmanga" (in Tangkhul), *The Legacy,* Vol. 4, No. 3, May-June 2006, pp. 8-11.
16. *Ibid.*
17. Singh, U. Dhananjoy. 2005. "Education: Its Genesis and Progress in Ukhrul District", *The Legacy,* Vol. 3, No. 3, May-June 2005, pp. 20-25.
18. Shimray, Y.K. 1988. *Lives to Remember,* Imphal: Published by Mrs. H. Shimray, p. 46 (The actual year of publication of these books remain unknown).
19. *Ibid.*, p. 76.
20. According to Y.K. Shimray the book *Tangkhul Miwurlung* was released from press four days after the death of Y.K. Shimray. So, he was not able to see the publication of this book (*Ibid.*, p. 77).
21. Chiphang, C. 2006. "Tangkhul Wordham Otmanga" (in Tangkhul), *The Legacy,* Vol. 4, No. 3, May-June 2006, pp. 8-11.
22. Shimray, Y.K. and Z. Maransa. 1993. *Tangkhul Literature Society Rinchan* (in Tangkhul), Ukhrul: Published by Tangkhul Literature Society, p. 12.
23. Luikham, R.K. 1957. *Chishutmi: Akhum II* (in Tangkhul) Ukhrul: Published by Rosalind Luikham, (Revised, Fifth Edition, 1988).
24. *Tangkhul Society Rinchan* (in Tangkhul) published by Tangkhul Literature Society in 1993 (p. 2).
25. *Ibid.*, p. 3.
26. In the idioms and perspectives of local people in Ukhrul, the attempt by INA soldiers to defeat the British colonial forces was generally understood as Japanese war. It was based more on the racial features and massive numbers of Japanese soldiers, who had invaded their territory.
27. *Tangkhul Society Rinchan* (in Tangkhul) published by Tangkhul Literature society in 1993, p. 11.

28. *Ibid.*, p. 25
29. Shimray, Y.K. 1978. *Tangkhul Poetry: Book I* (in Tangkhul), Ukhrul: Published by S. Haoreila.
30. *Ibid.*, p. 1.
31. The actual date and publication of this poetry has not been properly traced. However, currently it is part of Tangkhul textbook for Class XII, published by Tangkhul Literature society in 2001. *Wordham: Tuitam Kakhane (Class XII)* TLS Publication, 2001.
32. *Ibid.*, p. 99.
33. The exact date of publication remains uncertain and this novel remains unavailable.

3

Colonial Ideology and the Early 20th Century Texts

An Overview of Hegemony in the School Texts of Manipur

A.C. Kharingpam

The advent of different social and political theory in the recent past, such as post colonialism and post modernism have opened up a floodgate of understanding social theories and social paradigm in wide-ranging ways like never seen before in the history of mankind. Through these democratizing schools of thought, there have been growing realizations on the need to re-scrutinize and re-question the existing paradigm of education and its dynamics. In fact, the whole paradigms of social and political perspective have shifted. Through these new found perspectives, the once marginalized societies are now getting a fuller view of education and matrix of its functions in the society.

Educational practices and curricula do not take place in isolation, but are the result of human tendencies to influence, shape, impose and refine the existing practice. In fact, curricula are a result of some cases, determined by certain ideologies. Opining on the nature of education and its development in time, Zvi Lamm, in his essay, *'Ideologies and Educational Thought',* says:

> "In one of the early stages of the passage of societies from traditional to modern way of life – even before it was possible to define them as really modern societies – a change occurred

> in the legitimization of education. In traditional societies, this legitimization is mainly ritualistic. According to it, the accepted patterns of educational practice are good because they are accepted, or because they have always been accepted according to the common beliefs. Their acceptance granted them the status of basic facts of life, and anyone trying to change them was viewed as damaging and undermining these basics. Except for short periods of change in people's views, which were usually accompanied by crises, the individual living in a traditional society rarely faced alternatives of educational practice. His identification with the society in which he lived always included identification with one given type of education, accepted and even sanctified by the society, and – according to most of its members – the only possible and acceptable type. When traditional societies began to undergo changes, the ritualistic legitimization of education gave way to a new type of legitimization – the ideological legitimization of education." (Zvi Lamm, 1986, 1)

Thus, education involves the whole societal experience and experiment contained into a system that is legitimized by the narratives/poetics of the powerful known as ideology. To understand the nature of education and the system that provides the impetus, it is essential to recognize the relationship between ideology and education and the vital role ideology plays in the conceptualization and execution of education.

But it is essential to understand ideology before one analyses the role of ideology in education. 'Ideology' is an elusive term, which has been used in different periods with different connotations. In the past, the term had negative connotations, but in the contemporary times, it is used synonymously with 'philosophy'. 'Ideology', in simple words, can be defined as a set of beliefs, usually entertained at group levels. Ideology at group levels can be contrasted with individual opinions in a society.

Ideology constructs the stereotypes that are legitimised and supported by certain social institutions. Thus, ideology that has the backing of powerful social institutions becomes dominant in a society and has the potential to capture the minds of marginalised groups. It is this subtle hegemony of ideas, which was first focused and elaborated on by Gramsci in his work, *Prison Notebooks*.

Among other social institutions engaged in the process of socialisation, educational institutions and the intellectuals (Interpreters and framer of knowledge) play an important role in the construction and perpetuation of certain ideologies, which generally serve the interests of the dominant groups of the society. The well known observation by Gramsci that all men are intellectuals, and his claim that modern intellectuals were not mere speakers, but directors and organisers, who helped build society and produce hegemony by means of ideological apparatuses, such as education and the media, holds much truth in modern time. The distinction between a 'traditional' intelligentsia, which sees itself (wrongly) as a class apart from society, and the thinking groups, which every class produces from its own ranks 'organically' also reveals much about the nature of the positions occupied by different kinds of intelligentsias. The idea of creating an education system for the purpose of corresponding with the notion of critical pedagogy and popular education are later theorised and practised by Paulo Freire in Brazil, and have much in common with the thought of Frantz Fanon's proposal for the Algerians in his many works.

If we look at the history of education in Manipur we can see how education has been used to propagate certain ideologies favoured by the dominant culture and community. Although the indoctrination of ideological grain may not be as conscious and deliberate in the hands of the early western educationists, such as William Pettigrew, in as much as the purpose for educating the indigenous people of Manipur were concerned the intent remain the same – to create a subordinate class.

No ruler ever asked the masses for their choice or preference. They could make a decision on the part of others as they enjoyed power. The fact that every ruler tried to use education to legitimise and promote a certain ideology suggests the significance of education and its two-way relationship with ideology. This ideology of knowledge encourages a certain pedagogy, the sole objective of which is to transmit or pass on pre-existing knowledge from one generation to another. This ideology of pedagogical practices does not encourage any innovation, creativity or reflection. The students are considered passive recipients and the teachers become the engine to endorse the narratives of the state.

Since the beginning of human history, power has always been deployed in different ways. Yet the exercises of human power are always transmitted through discourses, which are embedded in various social structures and religious sanctions. This paper is an attempt to highlight the overarching elements of dominance in the early text books of the state of Manipur. The paper will also try to delve into the role of popular culture in normalizing and legitimizing the discourse of domination.

Thought the state of Manipur had its own history of rhetoric and literature even before the advent of the British, the arrival of the British in the state marked the coming of modern education in Manipur. As the British took control of the state in 1837, through the treaty of Yangdaboo, the colonial government took keen interest in introducing the natives to the new form of education, thus the first school of the state was established in the year 1872.[1] This was followed by the establishment of 12 new schools all over the state. As a result, by 1914, a few Manipuri students began to join the service of the British Government.

However, the aim of imparting education to the natives by the British was no different from what the British had conceived for the rest of India as mentioned above.

> *"We must at present do our best to form a class who may be interpreters between us and the millions whom we govern, a class of persons Indian in blood and colour, but English in tastes, in opinions, in morals and in intellect."* Thus, the primary objective of education was to produce good translators, who fear the might of the colonial power to interpret the colonial needs and wants.

The year 1894 heralded a landmark change in the history of western education in Manipur. The arrival of William Pettigrew to evangelize the Hindu Meitei and the ultimate unsuccessful attempt led to the spread of education in the hills of Manipur. Though Pettigrew could not convert the Vaishnavite Meiteis, his attempt to understand the language of the Meiteis led him to publish many books on the state and its language. The first work of Pettigrew was published in 1896 as soon as he reached Manipur. It was a translation of *the Book of John*[2]. The first Anglo Manipuri Grammar titled *Manipuri (Mitei) Grammar* was published in 1912[3] and by 1903, Pettigrew had published 23 school text books. In the years that followed, Pettigrew's attention ultimately charted toward the Tangkhul Naga language and the evangelization of the tribe.

On reaching the hills of the Tangkhul country in 1896, Pettigrew came out with a primer meant for the Tangkhul tribe in 1897. The primer was not only important as a document of western education for the Tangkhul, it became a colossal foundation of the demise of oral tradition and the beginning of written tradition in the annals of the tribes of Manipur. The introduction of the primer soon brought about phonetic changes in the language of the Tangkhul tribes and, gradually, the shifting of syntax and semantics. The publication of the primer was soon followed by *Luke wui Lairik,* a translation of *the Book of Luke* from *the Bible* in 1902. A collection of a few western hymns translated into Tangkhul dialect titled *'Jesu Wui La: Hymns in Tangkhul Naga'* was published in 1907. This marks the beginning of western musical culture in the history of Manipur. A dictionary titled '*Tangkhul Naga Grammar and Dictionary*' was published in 1918. The new dictionary not only tries to explain English to the students, but it also attempts to standardize meanings and pronunciations of the Ukhrul dialect for the entire Tangkhul regions. The first Tangkhul New Testament was published in 1926. Thus, the advent of western education was accompanied by the missionary's zeal to evangelize the native. This evangelizing approach brought about an uncompromising inclusion of Christian ethos and ideals in the curricula of the schools. Designed and written by Christian missionaries for missionarizing the people, the texts were replete with notions of western sense of history, education and superiority.

The result of such education system was that the first educated Tangkhuls could not help but abhor everything that was Tangkhul and Tangkhul sensitivity. A popular chorus sung by the first educated convert goes:

Mangkhama Hao nao bingna
Thingalungli khorum sai

(Laden with ignorance, the Haos
Worshiped stone and trees)

The underlying meaning of the above chorus reveals an overzealous, semi educated convert revelling in his new found identity as a man no more like his brethrens, but like the colonial teacher and reviling the culture to which he was born into.

Thus, the missionaries' emphasis on education for the indigenous tribals was rooted in the colonial belief and principle of 'civilizing the native' in order to create a new order in the likeness and convenience of the colonial power. As Musa Dube, the Botswanian Post-colonial feminist theologian aptly puts it:

> *"The modern colonizer... believed in the superiority of his religion, race, economy and culture. This superiority called upon the colonizer to bear the vocation of converting and ordering the world toward his own identity. Such an ideology was grounded in the belief of modernity, Christianity, and industrial advancement. The colonized..., on the other hand, were imbued with the belief that their own religion, race, economy, and culture were backward.*

Thus on reaching Ukhrul, Pettigrew, as expected, inevitably resorted to naming and placing the Tangkhul Nagas and their custom into colonial stereotypes, which was nothing less than dehumanizing and debasing the traditions and culture of the Tangkhul. Describing the people, Pettigrew noted that:

> *"Brethren in other hill stations will probably testify to the truth of this, and Manipur is far worse than any of the hill tribes – a fact which Government officials declare often... The missionary found the people anything, but truthful or reliable. The Manipuri is reckoned a liar, but these Tangkhul Nagas can beat him. The missionary has not come across one yet whose words or actions can be relied upon.*

Pettigrew not only portrayed the tribe as unreliable, but he also painted them as people '*like the rest of the Nagas of Assam, they are animistic in their worship, very superstitious and addicted to "zu" drinking to a great extent."*[4]

> *... They are naturally a cowardly set of people, susceptible to ridicule, and any suggestion of punishment frightens them.*[5]

Pettigrew's description of the Tangkhuls' social institutions and beliefs hinges upon the colonial understanding that everything native exonerates wildness and aberration.

> *"The villagers were independent and democratic; the chief and elders of each village were open to bribery and corruption, and had gained a reputation of being the biggest liars and biggest cowards among all the tribes of the state. Clannishness, the fear of spirits, a blind belief in the efficacy of monthly and annual feasts, ignorance, gross superstition, sin – all these held the people in thrall.*

Thus, the necessity of segregating and classifying the students/ converts was convincingly laid down by the missionary even as he began going about his missionary works. This act of separating the students from their community also helped the missionary to introduce Christian texts into the syllabus of the school without any hindrance from the parents and the Government.[6] The segregation of the new converts from the heathen society brought about a devastating effect on the social and political fabric of the tribe. Reports of clashes between the new converts and the villagers became a regular episode. However, with the total freedom given to him by the Government of Manipur, Pettigrew was able to successfully introduce and establish many schools within a short span of time. By 1906,[7] after much persuasion, a few women started attending the night School.[8] Pettigrew established the first girl's school in 1909, which was attended by 13 girls.[9] The following year, i.e., 1910, the Phungyo Baptist Church established the first women wing of the Church led by Alice Pettigrew and the girls, who graduated from the night schools.

Writing to the American evangelical ministry, Pettigrew wrote in 1899:

> *"No objection is made to Christian truth being taught. The boys are being taught in their own language and Manipuri. A few of them, who seem to have an aptitude for English, are being taught this language. The books they study aim to inculcate Christian truth. The school is opened daily with singing and prayer. On the Lord's Day, they come together for singing and to listen to the Gospel story. As soon as the Catechism is printed, they will be able to more efficiently retain in their minds the truths they have learned orally.*

Thus, education was tailored to cater to the needs of the missionary to evangelize the Tangkhul Nagas. It was through the medium of education that the natives could be connected to impart what was perceived to be right by the colonial power. It was through education that Pettigrew could succeed in taking home the message of the Bible to the people of the hills.

Pettigrew, being the superintendent of education in Manipur from 1895 to 1903, made full use of his position to imbibe and imbue the students into believing and accepting the principles needed by the missionaries and the colonial administrator.

Notes

1. In 1872, the first school was established at Imphal, however, it had to be closed down due to the lack of encouragement and suspicion from the Maharaja and the public (the Directorate of Education Manipur). In 1885, the Johnstone Middle School, Imphal, was established after many years of objections from the Darbar. As a reward of friendship and help in establishing the school, Sir James Johnstone agreed to address Thangal Major, Balaram Singh and Roma Singh Major as "General", (the History of Modern Manipur (1826-1946) edited by Dr. Lal Dena, 1990; History of the Christian Missions in Manipur by Karam Manimohan Singh, 1991).
2. William Carey translated a portion of the New Testament with the help of a Manipuri in Deb-Nagiri character in 1827 at Sirampore. It was published in 1831. However, no trace of the book could be found when the Pettigrews reached Imphal in 1894, *Baptist Mission Review*, Vol. XXXVIII, 1932.
3. A dictionary in English, Bengali and Manipuri by George Lawrie Gordon, 1837 later in 1888. A Manipuri Grammar, Vocabulary and Phrase Book to which are Added Some Manipuri Proverbs and Specimens of Manipuri Correspondence was publish by Arthur John Primrose.

4. Report from the Tangkhul Naga Field, 1899, Rev. W. Pettigrew.
5. A Tour among the Tangkhul Nagas, the Baptist Missionary Magazine, Vol. LXXXVII, 1909.
6. The curriculum in the valley school does not include Bible. Pettigrew was restricted from teaching any religious book by the Raja of Manipur and the British Political Agent for political reasons.
7. The Assam Baptist Missionary Conference Report, 1910.
8. A school designed by the Pettigrews to cater to the elderly. Classes were held at night, as it was the only free time for the farmers. Seeing the response of the women, Pettigrew established an all girls' school at Ukhrul in 1909. Phungyo Baptist Church Women Society Thotchan (History) 1910-2012.
9. The names of the first students of Alice Pettigrew were as follows: 1. Sanamla Ragui, 2. Harngaila Zingkhai, 3. Lasengla Rumthao, 4. Mahongai Rumthao, 5. Charani Angkang, 6. Ngalew Angkang, 7. Kasuni Angkang, 8.Asarew Sangkhro, 9. Shurila Muilung 10. Langzarla Raising (M.K. Shimray, *Tangkhul Miwurlung,* pp. 117, 118).

References

Bible Society of India. *Kathara Bible*. (Bangalore: BSI Publication, 1956).

_______. *The Holy Bible* (KJV). (Bangalore: BSI Publication, 1999).

Kanrei, T. *Wung Okthot Mayonza*. (Ukhrul: T. Kanrei, 1944).

Luikham, R.K. Chishutmi: *Akhum II (in Tangkhul)*. (Ukhrul: First published in 1957 by Rosalind Luikham, 1988).

Pettigrew, William. *Tangkhul Naga Primer*. (Ukhrul: William Pettigrew, 1896).

_______. *Tangkhul Naga Grammar and Dictionary* (Ukhrul Dialect). Shillong: Secretariat Printing Office, 1918.

_______.*Tangkhul Naga Grammar and Dictionary with Illustrative Sentences*. Ukhrul: The Tangkhul Naga Baptist Convention.1979 [reprint of 1918]

Tangkhul Baptist Long. Khokharum Laa. Ukhrul: Yarthot Publication, 1962.

TNBL. Kathara Bible, Ukhrul: Tangkhul-Naga Baptist Long, 1960.

_______. *Tangkhul (Wung) Dictionary* (Tangkhul-English).Ukhrul: Luikham, 1974.

Goody, Jack (1987): *The Interface between the Written and the Oral* (Cambridge University Press).

Hodson, T.C. (1919): Review (Untitled), *Journal of the Royal Asiatic Society of Great Britain and Ireland*, (Apr., 1919), pp. 249-253

Luikham, R.K. (1957): *Chishutmi: Akhum II in Tangkhul* (Ukhrul: Published by Rosalind Luikham, Revised, Fifth Edition, 1988)

Matisoff, James A. (1972): "*Tangkhul Naga and Comparative Tibeto-Burman*", Tonan.

Ajia Kenkyu, *The South East Asian Studies*. Vol. 10, No. 2, September 1972.

Ong, Walter J. (1982): *Orality and Literacy: The Technologizing of the Word* (Taylor and Francis).

Pettigrew, Rev. W. (1918): *Tangkhul Naga Grammar and Dictionary* (Ukhrul: Manipur Reprinted by Tangkhul Naga Baptist Convention, 1979).

Pettigrew, Rev. William (1899): 'Report from the Tangkhul Naga Field', The Assam Mission of ABMU.

Pettigrew, W. (1907): *Jesuwui Lâ: Hymns in Tângkhul Nâga in Tangkhul*, (Assam: Published by American Baptist Mission House, Ukhrul, Manipur).

Shimray, Y.K. & Z. Maransa (1993): *Tangkhul Literature Society Rinchan in Tangkhul*, (UKhrul: Tangkhul Literature Society).

Shimray, Y.K. (1988): *Lives to Remember* (Imphal: Mrs. H. Shimray).

Shimray, Y.K. & Z. Maransa (1993): *Tangkhul Literature Society Rinchan in Tangkhul*, (Ukhrul: Tangkhul Literature Society).

Shimray, Y.K. (1978): *Tangkhul Poetry: Book I in Tangkhul*, (Ukhrul: S. Haoreila).

Singh, U. Dhananjoy (2005): "*Education: Its Genesis and Progress in Ukhrul District*".

Solo, M. Jonah. Forty Years Mission in Manipur Mission Reports of Rev. William Pettigrew. Imphal: Christian Literature Centre, 2006. Chiphang, C. (2006): "Tangkhul Wordham Otmanga" (in Tangkhul).

The Legacy, Vol. 3, No. 3, May-June 2005.

The Legacy, Vol. 4, No. 3, May-June 2006.

4

Bankruptcy of Education

Ideology and Literature in the Context of Tangkhul Society

Yuimirin Kapai

That our education system is bankrupt hardly needs elaboration. Had there been a good education system or quality institutions, first, our students would have up-to-standard ability and, second, many of the parents wouldn't have sent their children to other universities, when most of them are weighing under financial problems. The truth is that majority of us would not have had the chance of either studying in good universities or of working in government services had there been no ST reservations. Despite the pressing needs, the absence of collective will and political act is an obvious indication of the refusal to assume ethical responsibility. It's time that we ask why we can't provide for our children an education system free from corruption and institutions capable of imparting quality education. The auhor attempts to examine the ideological underpinning of the education system, which is embedded in the social structure. With the theoretical framework so established, author looks into the phenomenal paucity of artists among the Tangkhuls and the pervasive philistinism (to use Mathew Arnold's term for the lack of artistic appreciation arising primarily out of the pre-occupation with materialistic values).

The Crippling Effect of Colonial Legacy

For the analysis of many of the present social issues, we often need to closely examine the forces of colonialism. We seem to agree that the effect of the colonial encounter was dramatic – "From darkness to light," "From head-hunting to heart-hunting." Yet we're also aware of the fact that the "transition" was not so smooth. Many of our forebears desperately held on to their traditions and beliefs, some till their last breath.

Somerset Maugham's short story "Rain" throws light upon the basic *modus operandi* of the missionaries. In the story, Mrs. Davidson, the missionary's wife, asserted that the first thing they had to do "was to put down the dancing," because the native dancing is "not only immoral in itself, but it distinctly leads to immorality." Besides dancing, she agrees with her husband that native costume "should be prohibited by law." Similarly, the missionary confessed that the most difficult part of his work was "to instill into the natives the sense of sin:"

> "You see, they were so naturally depraved that they couldn't be brought to see their wickedness. We had to make sins out of what they thought were natural actions. We had to make it a sin, not only to commit adultery and to lie and thieve, but to expose their bodies, and to dance and not to come to church. I made it a sin for a girl to show her bosom and a sin for a man not to wear trousers."

On top of making their "natural actions" sins, he made them punishable: "I instituted fines. Obviously the only way to make people realize that an action is sinful is to punish them if they commit it."

Indeed, Naga converts were forbidden from participating in "religious rituals and ceremonies, drinking rice-beer, dancing and singing folksongs and all sorts of amusements," in short, all "non-Christian festivals" (Lolly 44). In 1920, the observation of the Soul-Sending Festival (*Thisham Phanit*) practised by the Tangkhul was made punishable by payment of fine. The converts were asked not only to completely forsake their "old" ways of life, but they were also inculcated with the notions that their traditional "ways" was a source of shame. T. Luikham, a prominent early Tangkhul convert called his traditional customs "obnoxious." Lolly believed that the "strict discipline moulded the Christians to live a better social life" (46). By implication, without strict discipline, non-Christians led a degraded social life. Headhunting custom was identified as an irrefutable marker of Naga's barbarity and, therefore, a cause of shame. The image becomes firmly internalized among the Nagas that no less than a well-known Naga scholar M. Horam wrote, "The Tangkhul Nagas have rejected head-hunting completely and adopted a new way and advanced way of life" (88). In other words, the rejection of the "ignominious" custom is associated with an "advanced way of life" as opposed to the retrograde headhunting days.

To come to the point, creative activities, such as "dancing and singing folksongs and all sorts of amusements" were not only prohibited, but they were also made to be internalized as sinful and shameful. Not surprisingly then, our artistic creativity is smothered, aesthetic sense remains unrefined and a little of creative energy that we're left with is channeled towards religious concerns.

The Anomaly

Despite these powerful forces of change – colonial encounter and conversion – the basic social structure remains intact. And with it persist some traditional traits, in regard to education, an important one of which is paternalism. Drawing on Fei Xiaotong's classic study of Chinese rural society (and for the purpose of this paper), paternalism is simply defined here as "rule by elders": it includes the privilege to interfere against other's will for "greater cause," for instance, parental rights to send their children to school with or without children's consent for the good of the children. Paternalistic form of rule is encapsulated in such sayings as "Respect your elders," "Honour your parents."

Like Chinese rural society, the traditional Tangkhul society has paternalism, and in such form of governance, power is generated through patriarchal privilege and through education (Fei, 1948). Tangkhuls have a common saying: "*Fapai, harpai theikhare*." The claim to power, so to speak, is based both on age and knowledge. The association of age with knowledge and power found its way into the literature. In the tale "*Vāchap*," for instance, *Vāchap's* limb goes to the oldest, who is assumed as the wisest and powerful. In the myths of Naga's kinship with the plain people, whether it is Angami's relation with Assamese or Tangkhul's with Meitei, Nagas always insist that they are the descendants of the eldest. In the traditional society then, knowledge was indeed power. Even when formal education was introduced, the mode of instruction and functioning remained paternalistic. Just as it was in the traditional society, (cultural) education pervades the formal education. In the schools, defiant and sluggish students were treated like wayward children and they were sometimes subjected to appalling disciplinary punishments, such as, piercing of ear with thorns, flogging in front of other students, etc. Notwithstanding government policies and instructions, till date, corporal punishment and mental harassment are employed in educational institutions.

Regarding the upbringing of children, what Fei said of Chinese rural society may well apply to Tangkhul society: "The amount of correction a child gets in one hour would exceed the criticism an adult would receive in one year. To be a citizen under the most tyrannical king is no worse than being a child with the most loving parents" (116-117). Unlike a tyrannical king, however, what the parents teach is the culture itself. Besides technical training appropriate for a rural setting, children learn how to behave "according to the established cultural patterns, and how to manage the social roles embedded in group life" (117). Fei, however, observed that "The extension of educational power to relationships among adults requires a stable culture. A stable cultural tradition provides a guarantee of efficacy" (118). In a stable society, events seldom deviate from expectation and experience offers specific solutions for specific problems. However, when culture is unstable, traditional methods become inadequate to solve new problems and people can no longer rely on experience for guidance (119). In periods of social transition, then, when the paternalistic educational power oversteps the private sphere (where it does prevail) to pervade the public sphere (as it was in the stable traditional society), it habitually collapses in the face of new changes and challenges.

The primary purpose of education in the traditional society is to help children fit into the society so that they would serve the society and thereby serve themselves. Initially, formal education functioned likewise. Once upon a time, girls' education was considered adequate if they had learned how to read and sing in order that they might become literate choir members, and boys were expected to become an employee, preferably in the village, and support the family. Formal education as we now realize is hardly relevant to rural society. Therefore, most of the educated Tangkhuls are now living away from the hometown. The forces of globalization usher in not only the capitalist principles (which are progressively replacing the traditional economy), but also different cultural symbols and values (which are transforming our social life). Given the penchant for Western culture, powerful symbolic expressions of Western culture, such as language, music and images have long been part of our lives. Therefore, the culture of consumerism and the creed of individualism easily caught on in our society. Besides formal education, the inroads of such values and lifestyles are alienating young people from rural ways of life. The migration of our youths to cities needs to be seen in terms of the failure to meet the demands of their new values and lifestyles. Mercantile principle or market exchange for profit is increasingly attaining "a position of complete dominance over the economy and over the public and private experience." Instead of a means to a good life, market is becoming an end. Market and profit become an ideology (Hawkes, 1-2). The traditional social relation between men is being replaced by "a relation between things," or "a relation between monetary exchanges." Since money is the basic definition of value, the purpose of education has been largely narrowed down to personal accumulation of wealth. If I ask the students, who are helping us today, what they aspire to achieve through their education, I'm sure, most of them would want to secure a money-spinning job. Adults share similar attitude. An elder would claim paternalistic rights, but his privileges are no more employed to build society, but to build his own empire. The result of these forces of change is the process of what is called atomization, and its attendant effect of weakening social cohesion and disintegrating social solidarity. The rise of suicide cases and drug abuse are the signs of weakening social ties. In such different economic and cultural circumstances, the primary purpose of the traditional form of education is completely lost. In the realm of public sphere, paternalistic privileges have corrupted into becoming power without responsibility.

The basic argument here is: despite the enormous changes, the Tangkhul society is still characterized by an anomaly in which the traditional structural value system continues to determine and govern the education system. And by retaining the traditional traits, it still shows the basic sign of misrecognition – associating age with power or power with knowledge. Years of consequential misrecognition, I suppose, is the undifferentiated association of knowledge, power, wealth and status. That I have a respectable job (presumably therefore knowledge and status) doesn't mean I have wealth and power (particularly when power is misunderstood as the power to guarantee a job, funds, schemes, etc.).

The Discourse

In every society, there are always some sections of people, who stand to gain from the status quo, that is, from the social situation as it exists. According to classical Marxism, ideology is a set of discourse whose function is to justify and maintain the position of such sections of people. In the words of Karl Marx, "The ideas of the ruling class are in every epoch the ruling ideas." The individuals composing the ruling class act as "thinkers, as producers of ideas, and [they] regulate the production and distribution of the ideas of their age. Consequently, their ideas are the ruling ideas of the age" (93). However, the ruling ideas are not static, for the dominant group recreates itself and, by being alert to the shifting context, it adopts the worldview of the mass and makes it own. By doing so, the dominant group persuades the public to accept its own moral, political and cultural values. The mass, so to say, "lives" the dominant worldview as its own. It is certainly not Tangkhul's worldview (and perhaps not God's demand) that Baptist association is divided, nor is it in the interest of the common people that government funds and schemes are split among the *babus* and the so-called nationalists in the name of greater cause. However, we believe their views of Christianity or ideas of nationalism. This exactly is the function of ideology or what Antonio Gramsci called cultural hegemony: to make people believe in the ideas, which actually serve the interests of the dominant group as serving the interests of the people.

Despite the presence of print, now virtual culture, the principal medium of discursive formation is orality. In our culture, mass media is oral in nature. The significance of mass media cannot be overemphasized insofar as people gain most of their knowledge from it (Strinati 122). The readership of print media, such as *Aj* and *Legacy* is limited. Even in Delhi, owing to general apathy, publication of the student's magazine *Khānrin* and the fellowship's *Seihākhon* are erratic. And Delhi is supposed to be an intellectual center. Platforms for intellectual dialogue, such as seminar, conference, workshop and panel discussion are virtually absent. There is hardly any "informal" artistic group, such as drama, film, literature or media club, not to mention intellectual societies relating to historical, sociological and political interests, and scientific concerns. If there is any such group, which I'm not aware of, it must be focusing almost entirely on activism. Having been blackjacked by the system not to think and be critical, an intellectual space in Tangkhul society is still a dream.

In the absence of (print and electronic) mass media and intellectual activities, the most effective medium of discursive formation remains the Church pulpit. Usually, the pulpit is an exclusive preserve of priests; in the context of Tangkhul society, it has been made flexible. Thus, priests, theologians, bureaucrats, politicians, revolutionists, educationists, businessmen, social workers, in short, anybody, who is somebody, has an access to it. And by pulpit, I refer not only to the Church pulpit, but to a platform for any occasion with religious complexion. It includes fellowships, religious gatherings, religious functions (Christmas, Good Friday), rituals (marriage ceremony, condolence services), etc. The way I see it, pulpit is the most significant site of power; the pulpit in particular and the religious space in general is the site where power is formed, recognized and legitimized. It's not surprising then that our society values Church-goers and highly values orators. The prominent personalities are naturally eloquent speakers. Oratory is a skill, but it is not the only measure of intellect and orators can use their power for destructive purposes too. In our society, every important issue is taken up on the pulpit. Befitting the holy space, however, the issues have to be approached from the religious perspective. I believe it's not difficult to comprehend the supreme dominance of religion in Tangkhul culture. Recognizing the power of religion, the insurgent movement incorporates Christian practices into the organization, establishes its treasured slogan "Nagaland for Christ," and employs religious spaces to promote the movement.

Tragically, religion and nationalism can be abused and, historically, they are the most abused systems. God can be invoked to lend significance to any cause and the Bible can be interpreted to justify it. The rich around the world become rich through the exploitation of public wealth. More so in the case of the Tangkhuls: they are rich because they have pocketed the money meant for the people. Yet the rich have been justifying their wealth as the result of hard work and God's blessing. I haven't seen more hard-working folks than the country farmers, and yet they have been so indoctrinated as to believe that their destitution is the will of God. Leaders, no less the nationalists, can claim that their leadership is ordained by God in line with the logic of the erstwhile divine right of the king. I've often heard of underground leaders narrating how God saved them from the jaws of death. With a sense of self-satisfaction, they often concluded by claiming that God must have a plan for them [Meaning: God has a plan for them to be our leaders]. Well, who hasn't had a brush with death in one's life? In the words of writer Pearl Abraham, "When the highest value in a community is loyalty to the greater cause, meaning the continuity of the status quo, all means to this end are imbued with religious significance, and thereby justified."

Ideology and Tangkhul Textbooks

The present Tangkhul textbooks read more like some religious magazines meant to inculcate moral values in children than academic textbooks. When some points need emphasis or some actions justification, the writers liberally invoke God's name and His will. Almost all the chapters mention God and any achievement attributed to God. Even in a chapter on science – a dialogue on medical awareness ("*Phasa kaphā kala Tharkhamatheng*") – Dr. Chishutmi won't miss the chance to point out that God provides the means to keep healthy for human beings. Unmistakably, the syllabus committee is guided by this rigorous principle: to instruct and moralize the students.

The view that the function of arts is to teach (and to please) has a long tradition dating back to Horace's famous dictum: "The ultimate goal of poetry is to please and to instruct." Notably, Horace prioritized the function of pleasure to that of instruction. Sir Phillip Sidney and John Dryden reiterated the dictum. Interestingly, Dr. Johnson differentiated the function of poetry from other forms of writings ("The end of writing is to instruct; the end of poetry is to instruct by pleasing"), but he seemed to privilege instruction to that delight. The critical attitude changed profoundly towards the beginning of 19th century. John Keats practised the principle of what he called "Negative Capabilities," that is, capability to contemplate the world without the desire to fit contradictory aspects (uncertainties, mysteries) into closed and rational systems. He believed that poets should not be guided by the desire to impose his/her philosophy upon the readers. In modern literary theory, T.S. Eliot insisted that great poetry is defined by impersonality, for poetry is not an outpouring of personal emotion and experience, but the voice of tradition speaking through the poet. When the function of instruction is taken too seriously, Edgar Allen Poe exclaimed in exasperation by asserting that didacticism is a "heresy", which has corrupted "Poetical Literature [more] than all its other enemies combined." Arising out of the two World Wars, Holocaust, increasing domination by machines and widening gap of inequalities, the modern and postmodern literature show deep disillusionment with the traditional views of human rationality, dignity and goodness. Given the preference for intensity, complicated imagery, symbolism and allusions, on the one hand, and a new emphasis on impressionism, subjectivity, self-reflectivity and fragmented forms, on the other, modern and contemporary literature has long dismissed didacticism and rejected the concept of instruction and pleasure as a naïve and dogmatic approach to literature. At the risk of oversimplification, let me sum up the theories: what all these poets and critics maintain is that, firstly, the poet's philosophy, personality, beliefs and feelings should not be obtrusively present in his/her poetry and, secondly, the poet's emotion and ideas should not be directly described, but expressed through a vehicle of allusion, imagery, symbolism, etc. Keats illustrated with an example of "retired flowers," which would lose their beauty if they throng the street like some common prostitutes and cry out, "Admire me I am a violet! Dote upon me I am primrose!" What is valued in literature is not ideas *per se,* but "the concrete representation of thought." An essential quality of literature lies in showing something rather than in saying or explaining it. For literature appeals both to emotion and reason – something has to be left for "imagination," or at least arts must stimulate imagination and reasoning.

By way of an illustration, A.S. Akhui Zimik's poem "*Ngarumsak*" (Class IX) celebrates the value of co-operation not by telling, but through a metaphor of an event in which Garib Niwaz brought together the people of the hills and the plain to build a huge pond. Sometimes, the issue of what constitutes a good poem depends on the time in which it is perceived. Many of the poems in the Tangkhul textbooks might have been considered good poems in the Dark Age in Europe. Arguably, the notion of aestheticism must primarily be based on the critical tradition of a specific culture. So, appreciation of Indian literature must take into account the works of Bharata Muni, etc. or that of Chinese must keep in mind the works of Lu Xie, etc. Where is Naga's or Tangkhul's literary or critical tradition? None.

The poems and the stories in the Tangkhul textbooks are not devoid of artistic qualities, what they, however, share is "the heresy of didacticism." When everything that the readers ever need to know has been said, pointed out and explained, there is little left to imagine or ponder about. After reading them, what we're left with is seldom a challenge to our intellect or a sense of spiritual awakening or of deep feelings, but a nagging sense of dry moral truism.

Almost all the writings in the textbooks are interspersed with moral instructions and "experienced" counsels. Even such a fine poem as "*Titi-ot*" (Class VIII) ends with an injunction: *Lumlaolungli piphup khanuithot./T-Tangkhul, T-Tangkhul ot-sālu*. The first poem of the Class IX *Tangkhul Tuitam*, "*Ātamwui Shongza*," concludes with a line of counsel: "*Ātamli ngasoda ot solu*." In the last stanza of the next poem "*Chinaongara*" the poet exhorts, "*Leikashi hi semkāsa./ Wuklungwui pangshapna,/Katomkā ngaroksa*." The third poem "*Discipline*" declares "*Shimkhur*, School, *Yur kasem* discipline*li lei*." The fourth poem, "*Ngarumsak*," is a brilliant one, which nevertheless concludes with a moralizing stanza:

Katomlu makhararli,
Katomlu, akha eina akha,
Leisāra k lā mahai;

Maikhayā otsak kharum,
Mashimān katom'ngarok,
Tamkhuilu rakchithei'hai.

Except the last poem, all the poems and many of the chapters in the prose section are moralizing and sermonizing writings. It's equally true with the Class X *Tangkhul Tuitam*. The first poem "*Kathāna*" elaborates the qualities of leadership. The next one "*J khami*" is an elegant poem, but it is again a kind of literature, (again in the words of Keats) "which has a palpable design upon us," and so are the rest of the poems. Consider the titles of the poems in the textbooks of Class IX and X, "*Ngarumsak*," "*Ngaraikachā*," "*Ningkathar*," "*Pheokhami*," "*Atam Khamayon*," "*Mashun*," "*Na Mirin*," "*Kakhuiyali Khamiyana Kalā Mahaimei*." Clearly, all these chapters home in on instructing moral values. Listening to the lectures everyday must be like listening to ecclesiastical sermons and parental admonitions – now that I think of it, I shudder to imagine the classroom boredom.

Indeed, the textbooks aim to inculcate social values of the Tangkhul and general human values. Some great literary works are known for the representation of human values. Thomas Jefferson remarked that "A lively and lasting sense of filial duty is more effectually impressed on the mind of all sons or daughters by reading *King Lear* than by all the dry volumes of ethics and divinity that were ever written." Unlike Shakespeare's *King Lear*, the Tangkhul textbooks have the messages so overt and political that most of the poems and the stories become more like propagandist writings rather than what Rene Wellek called "Imaginative literature."

In a sense, the textbooks are true to our culture. In a culture dominated by paternalism and nationalism, and a culture, which regards highly of religiosity, generally speaking, literature (which is a cultural product) cannot radically depart from its ideology. Most aptly then, the speakers of the poems and the stories assume the voice of an authoritative patriarchal figure and put on the mask of a moralist, who always has to share some worldly wisdom and self-righteous morality. The poem "*Na Mirin*" (Class X) is a good example. The speaker of the poem, perceptibly an experienced elder well versed in the ways of the world, recreates the splendour of the youth, its beauty, health and audacity. By way of a refrain, he insists that life is not a caper in which festivity will only bring ruins, for humans live but once. So, today is "your" only time when "you" (students) should study.

> *Saikora hi ākhashima, khanishi maning.*
> *Māwon maphangluilākmara khanishida.*
> *Hao hao hā hā sak, mavāshung phei ngaphok,*
> *Aja kaho himana nawuivang katam kasha.*

The last stanza is reminiscent of Suisa's "*Huinākhar.*" It repeats the cliché, "As you sow so shall you reap":

> *Ayā ājawuivāngna, āja hi ākhama'wuivang.*
> *Aja shongza khangakhui okthotlung hili.*
> *Na ning matunrar, huinākhar theikakhui.*

What is realized when it's too late? I think the answer is obvious: wasting time in festivities and not studying hard enough. This blunt shallowness stands in stark contrast to such a profounder poem as "*Huinākhar*"; in "*Huinākhar*" the meaning of "a little too late" (*huinākhar*) is open to interpretations. When the answer is obvious, the message cannot be complicated: to pinpoint the message in a line from "*Ngarumsak,*" it is "*Tamkhuilu rakchithei'hai.*" In other words, the message of the poem is to learn what is taught and demonstrated ("*rachithei'hai*"), and not to find by oneself.

This message then characterizes Tangkhul culture. Children (who are considered not as individuals, but always as children) are dictated from above by the parents, elders and institutions; they are not allowed, let alone encourage, to decide for their own lives. What H.E. Stearns said of the 1920s American society seems to be quite applicable to our contemporary situation: "Something must be radically wrong with a culture and a civilization, when its youth begins to desert it... All our institutional life combines for the common purpose of blackjacking our youth into the acceptance of the status quo; and not acceptance of it merely, but rather its glorification." Naturally, Tangkhul society is highly ordered: women in the private space of giving birth, men in the public space of instruction, and children are the apprentices. If the order is maintained, wisdom would grow.

> *Avana onthomi.*
> *Tamena katommi.*
> *Naobingna shakhui'kha,*
> *Mirinwor chuikāra.*
>
> ("*Mashun*" Class X)

The epistle "*Naomayarli Chithi Kakapi*" (Class X) defines a good family as consisting of children who respect, trust and obey their parents, and indulgent parents, who nevertheless do not hesitate to chastise their children. And then it deliberates on what constitutes good manners and good character. As usual, the epistle concludes on a religious note by urging the son to first seek the kingdom of God. Many authors in the textbooks made it a point to state that great men love their parents. Sometimes, unimportant details are played up in order to point out paternalistic values. In a brief biography of Alfred Nobel (Class X), Alfred's father Immanuel is said to have lovingly cared for his wife and the children so much so that private tutors were hired and, thus, his children were well educated. Besides, Alfred is claimed to have no love affair till the age of forty because of his love for his mother. Some of Alfred Nobel's biographies that I've browsed do not bear out this observation: I wonder about the source of this information. It is not clear why Immanuel went to Finland and then to Russia in search of business prospects; nevertheless by doing so, he had to leave his family in Stockholm for five years. Hiring private teachers was not a luxury, and Immanuel had to hire because education was imparted in Russian, which his children could not understand. I'm not saying that Immanuel didn't love or care for his children, but I see nothing extraordinary about Immanuel's child-raising effort, which is worth emphasizing. However, in the context of the Tangkhul, it needs to be underlined that the love and concern showered by Alfred's parents and Alfred's love for and obedience to his parents ensured his success. This message is meant to reaffirm paternalistic order.

Sometimes, the didactic intention to maintain existing order is blatantly expressed as the last three lines of the poem "*Kathāna*" (Class X) show:

[*Kathāna michiva*]
Apreiva ākha khaleiya ningchānga,
Phālākeina shimkhur nganaoda ringa,
Āva lairik kathem, thangkhamei leiya.

The first line, "A leader aspires to have only one wife," endorses marriage institution and monogamy, which as Christians all of us would approve; but to assume that the institution of marriage and the practice of monogamy are unquestionable is to delimit what we can think and what we cannot. I believe everything should be brought within the sphere of our critical thinking. What is more upsetting is the chauvinistic assumption that a leader is a man (for a woman cannot have a wife). I'm sure the poet is not alluding to homosexuality, as husband and wife are terms applied to heterosexual partners. The second line legitimizes the status quo by suggesting that man has the highest responsibility in a family. Somehow, the notion again marginalizes women's role in a family. I find the last line equally appalling since "*lairik kathem*" is not an indispensable criterion of a leader, more so in the context of Tangkhul society. Besides, it implies an equivalence of "*lairik kathem*" and "*thangkhamei*," which is another form of misrecognizing between age and wisdom.

Nationalist ideals, bordering on chauvinism, do not lack behind. The poem "*Tangkhul Av ram*" sings in lofty praises of "Tangkhul Motherland": "*Tekkhamatei āvaram, yangla masānkachangma/... Tekkhamatei sāyur vāyur kala wonshivār saikora chi/... Haori-haorangna khangachān, nawui phungton/... Malāngluima āvaram Tangkhulli sāmi kahai.*" In "*Phasā kaphā kala Tharkhamatheng,*" Dr. Chishutmi affirms "*Ithum Tangkhul kaphung hiya Varena somikahai ramna …*" The poem "*Ningkathar*" (Class X) resounds with these words of glorification:

Masi, tara tharmei, shimmei
I Hao ramnao themmei, pingmei.
Varena sokhami ramli …

Tangkhul country is a nice place with temperate climate and suitable for many crops and fruits. But to claim it as abundantly blessed is a hyperbolic boast. In what way is there abundance? It seems to me, even Arunachal Pradesh surpasses in scenic landscapes. With regard to economy, Tangkhul country is sadly a landlocked area and a hilly terrain where industries and factories cannot be established. We feel a need to create an illusion of bounteous motherland, so that we may be inspired to love and protect it with our lives – it's a cheap patriotic propaganda.

"*Yur*" is a frequently repeated word, second only to "God": "*Yur hakkasang pong shongf* discipline *mana*" ("Discipline"), "*Yur-jātwui kahorna*" ("*Mashun*" Class X), etc. In a masterful stroke, the poem "*Ningkathar*" kills two birds with one stone by calling upon both the names of religion and nationalism:

Vare kala yur phaningda,
Mashun otsak tāzak sāda,
Sāmisa. sāman mathingla,
Ila, yurla, reisangchaora.

The poem identifies the service towards "*Vare kala yur*" as service towards oneself. In traditional society, as said, service towards society is a service towards oneself. In those days, society used to mean all sorts of relationships and interactions. Here, society is taken as the total sum of relations and interactions with religion and nationalism. The only poem that challenges and subverts the nationalist ideology is Ng. Woleng's prophetic poem "*J khami*":

Mi ākhamāngwui kaphaning
China mavaipaima.
...
Jakhami' mi mazangakha,
Khokha masāpaima.
...
Ningkhān ngatāntānlaga,
Ngasāthuihao mirao.

Some writings carry over the tradition of colonialist writing styles and its ideology. The personal narratives, "*Rokshirao Ramli Yaothuikhavā*" (Class X) and "*Ram Khayao*" (Class IX) follow not only the style, but the assumptions of colonialist travel writings.

Rokshiraoram (undeveloped country), like an oriental, is "a place of exotic beings, haunting memories and landscapes, remarkable experiences" (Said 1). The narrators, like the white colonial writers, are superior, civilized and knowledgeable, whereas the natives "others" are the opposites – inferior, uncivilized and illiterate.

Class VIII Course Book opens with L. Ragui's poem "*Zamshei Vaitei.*" The title as Ragui explains means finest, high quality drink, but strangely the poem talks about the damaging effects of alcohol consumption:

> *Mangsasang yotrei, yarkhoka malao suitur…*
> *Zamzā suisui khi ngatei f kapā.*
> *Zamshei vaitei kharom kazat naoshiyolong.*

The poem projects a serious misrecognition: it is not the traditional high quality drink, but the existing poor and unsafe drinks, which are the cause of misfortune. However, the poem seeks to trace back the present social ills to the traditional custom. The poem "William Pettigrew" paints a "dark" picture of pre-colonial Tangkhul society, which is alive with such customs as "feasts of merit" and honour-seeking warfare, and religious practices of worshipping stone. It denounces the honour system associated with such customs and practices. While wallowing in such dark world, Pettigrew opened their eyes to education and the gospel.

> *Matakkhak zingtunwui kahor phungra...*
> *I Hao tangkhulli mik rakranuda.*
> *Worrom rāpheisang, teokha leishiyei.*
> *Manglārin Kadhar rāyaosangmihai.*

The poem encapsulates the views of the older generation Tangkhuls, the custodians of paternalistic rights. According to this worldview, pre-colonial Tangkhuls practised "uncivilized" customs, abominable religion and followed repulsive habits. The west represented by Christian missionaries elevated the Tangkhuls from the state of utter "darkness" to the "light" of education and the gospel. In fact, these were the views of the west and, as generally agreed now, these views were employed to justify the inhuman exploitations and rules of the west over other peoples' nations. When viewed from today's perspective, most of the assumptions are true. Indeed our ancestors lived without any sense of hygiene; they were illiterate; they whiled away their time in festivities; usually their plan for future did not go beyond a year; they worshipped trees and stones, and so on. Situated as we are in our own cultural value system, we cannot understand the past unaffected by our present values any more than we can understand other cultures without being coloured by our cultural values. So the question is how far can we understand the past in terms of the time's value system?

I think, the horror of headhunting is overstated. There would be as many headhunting victims then as there are road accident victims today. The headhunting custom was inflated so as to project an image of lawlessness among the Nagas, which is ironic. Compared to the present situation, it was a highly ordered society governed by their system of honour. It is not the idea of killing a man that makes headhunting gruesome and repulsive, but the idea of what humans could do to dead bodies – for instance, cutting off heads, fingers, toes, sticking heads on the poles. Of course, our ancestors did not share such delicate sensibility. Besides, in the extremities of war, carefully drawn lines between civility and savagery often dissolve. At the end of the day, it hardly matters whether peoples are civilly shot or savagely beheaded. In feast of merit, rich people feasted the village and friends for days depending on the stage of the custom. During the occasion, the host spent family's wealth by killing as many buffaloes and pigs as the feast demanded. Certainly, it was an extravagant affair, wasteful if you prefer. However, the custom was consistent with their philosophy, which was, to live in the present. Therefore, they did not accumulate wealth for long, and the amassed wealth was shared among themselves, sharing of which was an honourable act.

Let us face it, with such oppressive institutions and status quo-maintaining education system, we cannot nurture creative minds, let alone produce artists. Compare our textbooks with NCERT's "Textbook in English for Class X." The first chapter has a short story called "A Letter to God" by G.L. Fuentes. In the story, a peasant named Lencho is worried because hailstorm has destroyed his crops. Finding no means to look after his family, he writes a letter to God asking for hundred pesos. When the postmaster reads the letter, he is moved by Lencho's faith in God. So he collects seventy pesos from the employees and sends it to the farmer. Lencho shows no surprise when he sees the money – "such was his faith." Counting the money lesser than he has asked for, he immediately writes another letter asking God to send him the rest of the amount and to deliver to him directly and not through the mail, because "post office employees are bunch of crooks." Simple as the story is, it has a powerful irony, which accentuates the theme of the story. The story raises important issues – faith in God, trust in humans, human nature, irony of life, conflict of humans and nature, and conflict between humans. There are no obvious easy answers, because the story depicts the complexity of human life. Along with the story, the first chapter has two short Robert Frost's poems; one of which is called "Dust of Snow":

> The way a crow
> Shook down on me
> The dust of snow
> From a hemlock tree
> Has given my heart
> A change of mood
> And saved some part
> Of a day I had rued.

Crows are scavengers and owing to its black colour, it's usually associated with death. In horror stories, they usually act as the harbinger of death. Whereas hemlock trees, the other symbol, are known for their toxicity. Of all the birds and trees, Frost chooses the fearsome crow to shake the snow off the poisonous hemlock tree, but they serve a delightful purpose: what would have been a gloomy day is saved by the beauty of the falling snow. The message seems to be that we should not judge the world with prejudice and stereotypes, for what is ugly can also bring beauty.

My point is that such story and poem encourage students to exercise critical thinking and thereby foster their creativity. Students should be pushed to ask question, to use imagination and reasoning. I wonder why classical poems, such as Rungsung Suisa's "*Huinākhar*" and Sanamla Ragui's "*Tui Sāri*" are not included in the syllabus of class IX and X. "*Tui Sāri*" is a celebration of "traditional wisdom," by which I mean the wisdom of the pre-colonial Tangkhul culture. In an inimitable style, Ragui yokes traditional sayings and aphorisms into a beautiful poem. The poem defies translation, precisely because the traditional Tangkhul worldview cannot be powerfully captured in terms of western culture. The poem, however, contradicts the paternalistic belief that the white people elevate us "from darkness to light." "*Huinākhar*" resists single interpretation, for it has multiple layers of meanings, which refused to be limited to a definite signification or single category. Is Suisa speaking about Naga's nationalism, or Naga's culture in general, or lack of historical consciousness, or of sense of community feeling? This poem again subverts monolithic worldview of paternalism. Conspicuously, folktales are also left out in the syllabus, perhaps, because they do not usually teach moral lessons and sometimes contradict Christian teachings.

Conclusion

Truly, the content of the Tangkhul textbooks abounds in useful information, wise words and moral values, which students will certainly need in their lives. What I find most inspiring about the textbooks is the emphasis on the sense of community – the feeling that one is a part of a community, the recognition of our interdependence and the willingness to maintain it (Sarason, 157). N. Luikham exhorts in "*Chinaongarā*" (Class IX)

> *Katomkā ngaroksa.*
> *Na lanla chungmeira,*
> *Kashimla shim-meira.*
> *Miyur hupta akhamāng.*

In an age so doggedly dedicated to personal profit, it is indeed an insightful observation to highlight that the development of a society is the development of its entire members. Furthermore, he goes beyond nations to embrace the world. B. Luikham in "*Ningkathar*" urges "*Vare mashunli pheisin sāda,/Ithum leishimei okthuisa.*" Many of the writers underline what A.S. Yereila asserts in the epistle,

"*Naomayarali Chithi Kakapi*," that since we've to live together, we must learn to live together.

However, as literary texts, it is worrying when they are all employed to affirm the existing value system and meant to inculcate conformism in the minds of the young people. Many great works of art are great because they dare to interrogate conventional wisdom, to challenge dominant values and to depart from the norms and conventions. Artists (and thinkers) of all ages explore the limit of human experience and, in the process, often confront dominant values. The experience enables them to imagine a new age. Every great civilization is, therefore, preceded and accompanied by an efflorescence of arts and literature (and new thinking). The might of Alexander is preceded by the writings of Homer, Aeschylus, Sophocles and Aristophanes, and that of Roman is accompanied by Plautus, Lucretius, Horace and Virgil, and that of British Empire by such writers as Chaucer, Shakespeare, Milton, Dryden, Coleridge, Tennyson and Dickens.

Public receptivity imparts a milieu where arts can flourish. R. Silas in "*Khangareo, Ngasamkakhui kala Otngashir*" categorizes reading novel, watching drama and film as a form of recreation. His view reflects Tangkhul's general attitude towards arts – that art is a leisure and a form of recreational activity. On the contrary, art is serious. The time engaged in artistic activities is not a time wasted. Though history abounds in artists, who struggled to the extent of paying with lives (Van Gogh), art is known to have flourished through patronage. The rich and powerful people, with an artistic consciousness and artistic bent of mind, can exist in a culture, which considers arts as a serious business.

As a rule, creative minds do not blossom in an oppressive environment. When the French monarchical rule stamped on the freedom of expression, Voltaire famously said, "I disapprove of what you say. But I will defend to the death your right to say it." Voltaire knew that if somebody controls what we can say, he controls what we can think; and if he controls what we can think, he controls our minds; if he controls our minds, he controls our consciousness, and a person without consciousness is no better than an animal.

References

First Flight: The Textbook in English for Class X. NCERT. 20/05/2013. http://ncertbooks.prashanthellina.com/class_10.English.FirstFlight/index.html>

Hawkes, David. *Ideology*. London: Routledge, 1996.

Horam, Mashangthei. *Social and Cultural Life of Nagas: The Tangkhul Nagas*. Delhi: B.R. Publishing Corporation, 1977.

Jones, Steve. *Antonio Gramsci*. London: Routledge, 2006.

Lolly, R.R. *The Baptist Church in Manipur*. Imphal, 1985.

Marx, Karl. *Selected Writings in Sociology and Social Philosophy*. Edit. T. Bottomore and M. Rubel. London: Penguin, 1963.

Maugham, W. Somerset. "Rain." 20/05/2013 <http://maugham.classicauthors.net/Rain/>

Pettigrew, William. *Forty Years in Manipur Assam: An Account of the Works of Rev. and Mrs. William Pettigrew*. Edit. Jonah M. Solo and K. Mahangtheio. 1986.

Poe, Edgar Allan. "The Poetic Principle." *The Works of Edgar Allan Poe Volume 5*. 20/05/2013 <http://www.gutenberg.org/files/2151/2151- h/2151-h.htm>

Said, W. Edward. *Orientalism*. London: Penguin, 2003.

Sarason, S.B. "Commentary: The Emergence of a Conceptual Center."

Journal of Psychology. Vol. 14: 405-407. 20/05/2013 <http://en.wikipedia.org/wiki/Sense_of_community>

Strinati, Dominic. *An Introduction to Theories of Popular Culture*. London: Routledge, 2004.

Tangkhul Tuitam Kachishata. TLS Publication, 2010.

Tangkhul Tuitam Kachiko. TLS Publication, 2010.

Tangkhul Tuitam Kathara. TLS Publication, 2010.

Xiaotong, Fei. *From the Soil: The Foundations of Chinese Society*. Trans.

Gary, G. Hamilton and Wang Zheng. University of California Press: Berkeley, 1992.

5

Traditional Knowledge, Social-cultural Practices and Modern Education

Tuisem Ngakang

The study of Nagas' colonial history has been dominated by the establishment of British rule, the spread of Christian mission influence, the development of nationalism, and the socio-cultural changes that transpired as a result. Though colonial rule lasted only for 69 years[1], its imposition had a drastic effect on Naga societies. Colonial initiatives, such as Christian missions, western style education and the introduction of a *lingua franca* transformed the Naga societies and it radically altered the socio-cultural fabric of the Nagas.

In this paper, I shall focus on the impact of modern education introduced by the Christian missionaries on the socio-cultural aspects of Naga. The influence of Christian missionaries is manifested in every aspect of Naga life. Thus, there are good reasons to begin with missionary activities in the case of the colonization of the Nagas. Christian missionaries represent the most naïve and, therefore, the most intrusive and transformative facet of colonial life. Administrators aimed at limited ends, such as law and orders, taxation, etc. the missionaries invariably aimed at transformation in the beliefs and actions of native people, at colonization of heart and mind as well as body. In pursuing this sustained policy of change, the missionaries demonstrated a more radical commitment to rule than the political administrators did.

The paper will be broadly divided into two parts; the first will deal with the pre-colonial set up of traditional education and method of transmission of age old traditional knowledge. The second part of the paper will focus on the motives behind the introduction of modern education by the Christian missionaries and its impact on the socio-cultural tradition of the Nagas.

The paper will try to conclude with a few suggestions, which I feel necessary, in sustaining and continuing the rich cultural heritage of the Nagas.

Pre-colonial Set Up

In a tribal society like that of the Naga, every aspect of life was interlinked. Change in one aspect disturbed the whole structure of life. The stopping of head-hunting, which was the centre of social and religious institutions, which shaped the lives of the Nagas, had a direct impact on the disappearance of the *longshim/morung*[2].

In every society, the child is born naked, untaught, bestowed only with his instinctive qualities of mind and body, and they have to gradually acquire the skills and the ideas of his culture and to develop moral values, social attitudes and the beliefs.

In the society like Nagas, this whole process of education is carried on by the family and later by the play/work group in the *longshim* (morung). In addition to the myriad functions of the *longshim*, it was one of the most important community institutions, where age old culture and traditions of the society were imparted. In other words, *longshim* served as a school in the absence of any institutionalized system of schooling. It is here that the foundation of each generation are laid, moulded and built up. *Longshim* was the only place where the heroic deeds and valor of the earlier generations are taught and, thus, it is the glory of the past from which the seeds of the future have to sprout.

Through the *longshim*, young people get acquainted with the history, culture, folklore, songs and dance of their village. M. Alemchiba Ao, writing on the functions of morung (*longshim*) wrote that it was here that lives had been moulded to fall in line with the Naga way of life. Here, they learnt the advantage of cooperation and responsibility. They became more self-reliant, with common sense, and better disciplined. It is here that their loyalty and sense of service to the community was developed[3].

The indigenous Nagas educate their children through the on-going process of life in their traditional customs and values. Through their traditional tales and myths, the elders teach the children the moral, ethical modes of behaviour and social organization. Through certain religious rituals and practices, communal attainments of spiritual ideals are established. From birth, through stories and legends about survival, endurance and respect for nature and all mankind, children are taught. Toys and playthings are fashioned for them, including tools and traditional dress, so that they may learn early about the roles they will assume.

Girls were provided with packing parkas and carried their dolls on their back just as they would carry their children in the future, and they were taught the traditional styles and methods for sewing and designing clothing. Boys were dealt with from an early age as budding warriors, and were introduced to traditional games, group play and exercises to learn alertness, improvisation and endurance.

Folk songs were one of the medium through which education was imparted in the absence of institutionalized schools in the Naga society. (Informal education occurs in a spontaneous, unplanned way. Formal education is a purposeful, planned effort to impart specific skills or information. Formal education is a systematic process in which someone designs the educating experiences). The simple tunes and straightforward songs enlighten the tender minds of children with the useful knowledge of geography and history in the earliest manner. The moral song teaches the young people the norms and conduct of heroes, method of building the houses and technique of agricultural activities.

These spiritual ideals laid the foundation for respect, which the indigenous Nagas have for their political and social institutions; the love respect and obedience, which the children must show to their parents and elders; the strong loyalty to oath and the restraints from the perpetuation of evil within the society. Through cultural participation, children acquire the techniques of communication.

The transmission of the knowledge on the one hand is incidental rather than making a conscious decision to learn them. He initially learnt the cultural aspects of the society as an incidental part of association with his father or mother or absorbed the information from the senior inmates in the *longshim*. For the Naga society, story telling and singing are more than exercises for entertainment and passing away the time. It is a sacred trust that the old man must pass on before he dies.[4] On many occasions, in rainy seasons or in cold winter noons, old men were usually surrounded by curious wide-eyed children and adults, enjoying the long session of story telling and singing till late nightfall. On festive occasions, boys and girls of different age-groups join the elders members of the village in singing. Children watch the verbal and gesture expression of the elders and repeat them.

Colonial Encounter

There is a general agreement that the spread of modern education has been one of the most powerful forces in Naga social changes.

Education in the modern sense of the term was first introduced by the American Missionaries to the Nagas. Before the coming of the formal missionary education, proper classrooms, blackboards and white chalks were unknown to the Nagas. However, the kind of education given to the Nagas was only to serve the missionaries' need to evangelize. The Government had its own agenda in supporting missionary education; they considered education as the best agency to introduce the rugged Nagas to order and civilization.[5]

From the very beginning of their contact with the Nagas, the British officers identified the necessity of introducing western education. They saw education as the best means of 'civilizing' the rugged Nagas[6]. The education of the 'heathen' was essential to missionary work from the beginning, and Baptist missionaries stressed the importance of a thorough knowledge of the Bible by the faithful. Education went hand in hand with religious works. Christianity and education became closely related. Puruthenpurakal observed that, "In the course of a few years, schools and boarding became the chief form of evangelization of the Naga people. Perrine and Down in the Ao areas, Rivenburg and Supplee among the Angamis became the main promoters of this singular means. All other missionaries in some way or other were 'school men' and did what they could to improve the station schools and the schools in various villages. Out of them came teachers and preachers, who formed the big array of native evangelists on whom depended to a large measure the success of the evangelical work in the Naga Hills."[7]

The entire teaching staff was Christian and books and other teaching aids were selected or developed by the missionaries. Religious instruction was especially stressed in schools. In the initial stage of the introduction of education, Naga parents were reluctant to send their children to missionary schools for fear of conversion to Christianity. As late as 1937, the government stated its view on missionary schools: "...while acknowledgement must be made of the debt owned to the missions for their work as pioneers in the field of education, it must be recognized that the missions have interested themselves in education solely with the object of Christianizing the children. Portions of some of the hill tribes have refused education, because it brought Christianity with it, and it is unfair that they should be deprived of education because they are unwilling to abandon their tribal custom."[8]

The main objective of schools was in fact the proclamation of the Gospel, the first convert were usually from the schools. The logic behind their interest in schools was driven by the conviction that they would help spread the Gospel[9]. The missionaries were anxious that the best pupils of the village schools, when admitted to a higher school were trained in evangelical work in the village as teachers and interpreters. In fact, the success of evangelization in Naga areas depended to a large measure on the schools and their hostels.

The educational opportunities offered by the missionaries evoked little enthusiasm at first. Parents frequently had to be convinced by small sums of money or presents of clothes to send their children to school. When the need arose, the missionaries and government officers even used force for conversion. In Ukhrul in 1896, when Rev. William Pettigrew, the first missionary in Manipur, persuaded the villagers to send their children to school, they were unwilling to do so. So the reverend informed the Political Agent of Manipur to take action against the villagers. The Political Agent promptly threatened to burn down the village and flog the parents in a bid to force them to send the children to school[10].

People took real interest in western education only when colonial rule was firmly established and the money economy had grown in importance. Nagas became aware that to be able to read and write meant tangible material benefits and opened up the possibility of cash income by working as a mission helper, teacher, government clerk, etc.[11]

M. Alemchiba, writes that the mass education started in the area only after Indian independence. He shows that in the Naga Hills, the percentage of literacy even as late as 1941 was only 5.09 which rose to 10.39 and 17.91, respectively in the years 1951 and 1961. With the introduction of the central scholarship scheme for ST, SC and the OBC, a considerable number of students could go for post-matric studies and by the end of the 1950's, there were several hundreds of matriculates and nearly 300 graduates and post-graduates in different fields.[12] Colonial education can be summed up in the words of the report on the Northeast Frontier Agency of June 1944, "No education policy has yet been laid down and the matter will require very careful consideration. Our present system is clearly gravely defective when applied to primitive tribes, for it tends to affect the individual rather than the community and, instead of making the individual more fitted for his community, it separates him from it and causes him to seek a living elsewhere, with the result that such good as he may have received is not ordinarily passed on by example to his fellow villagers".[13]

Among the Tangkhul Naga, the first school was opened by Rev. Pettigrew on February 19, 1897 with 24 boys. Initially not a single boy in the school was ready to embrace Christianity. However, by 1901, 12 boys agreed to be baptized. William Pettigrew, commenting on the conversion of the boys wrote: "The first fruits of the mission – the first fruits of the school."[14] The nexus between the mission school and conversion was obvious. William Pettigrew further wrote that, "The writer has found from the church and school records that quite 95 per cent of the scholars, who have passed through this school for either short or long periods, have become Christians."[15] Besides the school curriculum, the missionaries organized various evangelistic activities among the students in the village. Student's conferences were organized occasionally on Biblical themes; village tours were organized by student Gospel teams, scripture classes were given, all with the purpose of conversion. The census of 1911 shows that the proportion of literates was the highest among the Christians.[16] Various mission centers along with educational institutions were established across Naga centre, which was opened at Molungimong village in 1876, served the Naga tribes of the Aos, Sangtams, Changs, Phoms, Lothas and Semas, respectively for schooling, evangelisms and in training the young natives of the region in Biblical education. The Kohima Mission was mainly instrumental in imparting education as well as training to the Southern Naga tribes consisting of Angamis, Chakesang, Maos, Zeliangrongs, Rengmas[17].

From the beginning, the missionaries saw its new literate converts not as fodder for a growing administrative[18] organization, but as new missionaries prepared to convert their fellows. The new converts were sent to evangelize fellow villagers. The aim and objective of mission schools was summed up in the reports of E.W. Clark, the first missionary in the Naga Hills.

"The main object of these schools is the proclamation of the gospel to the people of a village where the teacher is located. The first converts are usually from the men of middle life. Later, as the children grow up, we reap from the schools; and as these know how to read the scriptures, we have a better foundation for church-membership and for preachers. At school, two hours in the morning during week days does not seriously interfere with the teacher's work as preacher during the rest of the day. Our reliance for the formation of Christian character is upon the spirit and the word, not upon secular education."[19]

The textbooks for the schools were mostly translated or written by the missionaries. The missionaries prepared grammars and dictionaries and translated the Gospel. Hymn books and catechisms were designed for the students.

Because of the difficulty involved in translation work and the absence of scripts in tribal languages, the government readily accepted the available books for use in schools as textbooks.[20] Translated Biblical texts were taught in schools. Translated hymns were used as texts both in school as well as in the religious services.[21] The classes usually began and ended with prayers and hymns. Rev. R.B. Longwel, one of the missionaries who stayed in Ao for 21 years from 1906-1927, wrote:

> "Not education, but evangelization, was to follow. It was not to be secular, but of a strict religious nature. The lessons were not in algebra, geometry and foreign languages, but in the observance of the Christian mandates. It was so for the very best of reasons, that "the fear of the Lord is the beginning

> of wisdom", unless evangelization precedes education, it will have an immeasurably greater task to perform after the world has been educated.....Christianize a nation and they will educate themselves."[22]

The students were taught to emulate and admire Biblical heroes like Abraham, Isaac, Jacob, Moses, who were great men and women of the Jewish nation in the ancient world. The author, himself a Naga Christian, grew up singing *"Father Abraham has many sons, many sons has father Abraham, I am one of them, so are you, so let us praise the Lord*"!! Odd though it was for Naga boys and girls to call Abraham or Jacob their father or look upon Jerusalem as their holy city, the strategy worked. Naga history was undermined and the indigenous traditional culture ceased to appeal to the imagination of young Nagas.

These educated were the first to drift away not only from traditional occupations, such as agriculture, but were also the first to become alienated from their traditional culture. The missionaries did their best to stop students from becoming involved in communal ceremonies or other traditional and cultural activities. From the beginning of their enrolment in missionary schools, Naga students began to be estranged from their own community. They began to hold their traditional heritage in contempt. Instead of teaching students of the significance and meaning of Naga custom, ideas and institutions, the missionaries taught the student to stay aloof from all indigenous activities. The obvious outcome was of the growth of a culture of self-hatred and a loss of pride in being a Naga.

Western missionary education was the most effective agent of deculturalization. The missionaries were indifferent to Naga culture from their first contacts with them. Mrs. Clark, the wife of a pioneering missionary in the Naga Hills, wrote that when she first met the Nagas, they "... entered a corner of India "...where the darkness seemed impenetrable."[23] She spoke of "savage worship and strange legends;... representations of men, elephants, tigers and leopards, skins of hornbills, lizards and snakes, and skulls – human and imitation – which filled the Naga houses as decorations created an uneasy feeling; warriors with battle axes and spears were an ordinary sight; village feuds and village raids were common, in addition to head-hunting expeditions."[24]

The missionaries believed that it was their Christian duty to root out the "pagan practices" of the Nagas without taking the trouble to understand the logic of Naga customs. Their main instruments for rooting out indigenous Naga practices were the schools they ran. The main aim of these mission schools was the proclamation of the Gospel, and school children were usually the first converts. It became a precondition for conversion that school children had to give up their indigenous culture before becoming Christians.

We must remember that, practically all education in Naga areas was started by missionaries and that even up to the present, it still remains almost exclusively in missionary hands. For this, the Nagas owe evangelism a deep debt of gratitude. This fact, however, had important historical consequences. Naga education before colonial conquest and the arrival of Baptist missionaries was an informal system, but it was practical and vocational. Every household was an educational institution; children were educated by the parents to be good warriors and responsible housewives. Home schooling was reinforced by the dormitory where both boys and girls learnt social customs on their own.[25] In Naga society, the process of education is conducted by the family or the play group, through initiation, ceremonies and apprenticeship. In contrast to this intimate tribal education, missionaries' education removed the individual from family, playmates and peer groups to specialized institutions.

The impact of colonial modernity led to the introduction of a regimented, schematized system of western education known as "schooling". The school curriculum was formulated and fashioned according to western cultural ideals and values.[26] Very little reference was made to indigenous Naga knowledge or values. Formal western education deculturalizing the Nagas, and in 1961 Verrier Elwin observed that the modern education substantially changed the socio-cultural life of the Nagas.[27] Curiously, Nagas weren't taught the classical culture of the West. Missionary education didn't teach Socrates, Plato, Mozart, Beethoven or Lizst. Their education was confined largely to basic literacy and Bible knowledge. Thus, with the introduction of education, literate Nagas began to drift away from their own culture without being initiated into the European high culture.

Conclusion

In the conclusion, allow me to point out a few points, which I feel necessary, in sustaining and continuing the rich cultural heritage of the Nagas. We need the kind of education that nurtures the understanding of the links between person and land, between local heritage and global civilization; students should learn to explore the meaning of rural life, and maintain their attachment to the community. Only through strong roots with the community, it will be possible for young people to contribute to community development while achieving personal success.

The educated Naga must be taught in such a way that he will not be unmindful of his indigenous cultural traditions and heritage. He must be taught to understand the meaning, values and significance of the indigenous cultural traditions and customs. Such an educational process will help in instilling in the Nagas a sense of the new cultural pattern.

Every school should take an initiative and facilitate periodic competitions based on the indigenous cultural tradition. These competitions could engage traditional story tellers, who are the experts in traditional customary laws, folk dancers and singers as well as experts in indigenous cuisine, pottery, cloth weaving and so on, for the purpose of enhancing skills, promoting a competitive spirit and creating general awareness of the rich heritage of the Nagas. The winners should be handsomely rewarded and celebrated.

The existing schools and institutions may also consider organizing "summer camp" inviting experts from different associations to teach school children the tradition of indigenous Naga cultures (like bamboo/cane craft, wood carving, cloth weaving, pottery, indigenous dance, drumming, storytelling, etc.), which they are not likely to have learned within the confines of regular school education.

Similarly, there is a need for a general revision of the existing schools syllabi in order to accommodate the cultural heritage of the Nagas. The teaching of culture and tradition must begin at home and must continue into primary as well as secondary education. School curricula must be made to reflect the necessity of cultural values and national pride. Such curriculum must be capable of giving the Naga child a new and positive consciousness of self as a Naga.

References

1. Officially, the British occupied Kohima, the heart of Naga Hills on 14th November 1878 and continued its rule till India got independence on 15th August 1947.
2. Morung is of Assamese origin, now commonly used for bachelor's dormitories. Every Naga tribe had a name for bachelor's dormitories, the Ao Naga call 'arichu' the Tangkhul Naga call 'longshim', the Angami call 'kichuki', the Sema Naga call 'dekha chang', etc. The term 'Longshim' for dormitories is used by Tangkhul Nagas, derived from two words i.e. 'long' means group and 'shim' mean house. Longshim, thus, is a group-house where boys and girls have to live and sleep from the time they get themselves admitted in that organization.
3. Alemchiba Ao, *Problem of Re-adjustment to New Situation (with special reference to Naga tribes)* K.S. Singh (ed.) *Tribal Situation in India.* Christopher Von Furer-Haimendorf *says that the bachelor's hall is an institution much like the English public school. The Naked Nagas,* p. 53.
4. M.Horam, *Social and Cultural Life of Nagas (The Tangkhul Naga)*, B.R. Publishing Corporation, Delhi, 1977, p. 51.
5. For. Deptt. Pol-A, May 1840, No. 148.
6. For. Deptt. Pol-A, May 1840, No. 148.
7. Puthenpurakal, *Baptist Mission in Nagaland*, Firma KLM Pvt. Ltd., 1984, p. 143.
8. *Quinquennial Review of the Progress of Education in Assam*, 1917-1922, p. 63.
9. In the beginning, the main object of the government in supporting the schools was seen as a part of the pacification programme. Later on, it has become a cheap way of performing a service for the government. The government reaps the harvest from the literate Nagas to aid them in performing administration works. Thus gradually, consciously or unconsciously, the mission work helps in strengthening and establishing the foreign rule.
10. S. Kanrei, *Hunphun Thotrin Chan* (Hunphun History), 1967, p. 143.
11. Joseph Puthenpurakal, *Baptist Missions in Nagaland*, Firma KLM, Pvt. Ltd., 1984, p. 143.
12. M. Alemchiba, in K.S. Singh (ed.) *Tribal Situation in India*, 1986, p. 483.
13. Home Dept., File No. 31/15/45, June, 1944
14. *Rev. William Pettigrew, My Twenty-Five Years 1897-1922 at Ukhrul Mission School*, p. ix.
15. *Ibid.*, p. vi.
16. *India Census, 1911, Assam*, Vol. 3, p. 1, p. 87.
17. Down F.S., *The Mighty Works of God: A Brief History of the Council of Baptist Churches in North-East India: The Mission Period 1836-1950*, Christian Literature Centre, Guwahati, 1971, pp. 95, 137

18. *However in most cases the government also reaps from the mission schools to fulfill their administrative needs.*
19. *The Baptist Missionary Magazine*, Vol. LXVIII, Feb. 28, 1888, p. 62.
20. *Quinquennial Review of the Progress of Education in Assam*, 1907-1012, Vol. 1, p. 121.
21. 5th Triennial Conference, Dibrugarh, February 11-19, 1899, Quoted by Milton S. Sangma, 1992.
22. Baptist Missionary Magazine, 1909, p. 170.
23. Clark, M.M., *A Corner in India*, C.L.C., Gauwahati (Reprint), 1978, p. 162.
24. *Ibid.*
25. Ghosh, B.B. *Gazetteer of Nagaland, Mokokchung* Dist. p. 72.
26. Instead of encouraging the Naga traditional folk tales, Aesop's Fables were printed and taught in the missionaries' schools. In 1941, G.S. Supplee, reported in *Missionaries Conference, 38th Session*, Golaghat, December 4-9 that Aesop's Fables were sent to the press for printing.
27. Elwin Verrier, *Nagaland*, Shilong, 1961, p. 78.

6

Curricula and Education System of Manipur State

Ringkahao Horam

Manipur is racing along with India in the world of progress, yet it is lacking far behind in many fields, particularly in education. If education is a journey of life, then the syllabus for the student is the roadmap of the journey. A carefully planned, clearly written comprehensive syllabus is one of the most important resources we need to provide to the students. A well-designed syllabus can provide knowledge more effectively to the student. The syllabus and the education system in Manipur is not systematically planned nor does it cover the unique social and cultural heritage, particularly of the tribals. The imposition of some of the dominant group's language, culture, etc. is vividly seen. Moreover, the government's lack of education policy and ineffectiveness in dealing with corrupt practices in the Education Department is decaying the education system in Manipur.

India is a country racing with the world progress. Yet, it is lagging far behind in many fields including education, particularly in the Northeast region of India. It has many reasons; some of the problems of the syllabus and education system of Manipur are discussed in this chapter.

If education is a journey of our life, then the syllabus for the student is the roadmap of the journey. A carefully planned, clearly written, comprehensive syllabus is one of the most important resources one can provide to the students. A well-designed syllabus performs much functions for the instructor and for the student. It outlines course expectations, organizes information, sets the tone for class interaction and guides student's learning. A skilfully detailed and designed syllabus can provide good education to the student. After all, education is the root of our life. George Sabine said, "If virtue is knowledge, it can be taught, and the educational system to teach is the one indispensable part of a good state. From Plato's point of view, with a good system of education, almost any improvement is possible; if education is neglected, it matters little what else the state does" (Sabine 1973: 69).

Teaching and learning do not take place in a vacuum. Within the context of the class room, effective teaching and learning requires partnership between the teacher and students. And in this aspect, the parameters of the relationship of the students and teacher need to be clearly defined and the responsibility assigned to each party be honestly and sincerely articulated. Only then, it can bear fruit. Prof. Yash Pal said, "Education is not a physical thing that can be delivered through the post or through a teacher. Fertile and robust education is always created, rooted in the physical and cultural soil of the children and nourished through interaction with parents, teachers, fellow students and community" (National Curriculum Framework, 2005).

Plato, in his proposed scheme of education, makes certain assumptions:

(i) Soul, being initiative and active, throws up, through education, the best things that are latent in it;

(ii) Education moulds the character of the growing young; it does not provide eyes to the blind, but it does give vision to men with eyes; it brings soul to the realms of light; it activates and reactivates the individual;

(iii) Each level of education has a preassigned function: the elementary education helps individuals give direction to their powers; middle level education helps individuals understand their surroundings; and higher education helps individuals prepare, determine and decide their course of action;

(iv) Education helps people earn a living and also helps them to become better human beings. (Arora, 2012: 12.9)

The National Curriculum Framework 2005 of NCERT proposes five guiding principles for curriculum development, which are:

1. Connecting knowledge to life outside the school;
2. Ensuring that learning shifts away from rote methods;
3. Enriching the curriculum so that it goes beyond textbook;
4. Making examinations more flexible and integrating them with classroom life; and
5. Nurturing an overriding identity informed by caring concerns with the democratic polity of the country.

Prof. (Dr.) Vicki Casella, an eminent scholar, said that while developing syllabus the following items must be considered and included.

- Instructor information
- Course information
- Method of instruction
- Course description
- Course objectives
- Course calendar or schedule
- Course policies
- Text book supplies
- Assignments
- Grading, etc.

He further said that syllabus act as:

I. A roadmap to guide the teaching and learning process.
II. Organizational tools to help manage the teaching and learning process.
III. A contract to ensure that all parties are clear on the expectations and responsibilities associated with the course.

The primary object of education as per Plato is "to turn the eye, which the soul already possesses, to the light. The message, which Plato conveys in this metaphor is that the whole function of education is not to put knowledge into the soul, but to bring out the best things that are latent in the soul. Plato thinks that human soul is repressive to its environments. But how it will respond, education teaches that, soul is sometimes ill-nurtured and ill-trained and education places it on a proper footing" (Das, 2013: 38).

I do agree with Venkata Rao in his book 'Ancient Political Thought' where he said, "Plato was the first person to formulate a university course. He was perhaps, the first person to speak of education, exclusively provided by the state. Anything of crucial importance should not be left to private initiative. In Protagoras, Plato criticized the shortsightedness of the Athenian parents in entrusting the education of their children to the sophists. He stoutly maintained that there is a far greater peril in buying knowledge than in buying meat and drink. Since education is very important, the curriculum must be controlled and defined by the state (Venkata Rao, 2002: 59).

Plato, the greatest idealist political thinker explains minutely about the curriculum of education. His educational curriculum could be broadly divided into two stages – Elementary and Higher. The elementary or basic education was further sub-divided into three stages. The first stage was from birth to the age of six years. At this stage, to both boys and girls, Language and some of the basic facts of religion were taught. At the second stage from six to 18 years of age, children were taught music and gymnastics. Music was essential for the development of the soul and gymnastics for the development of the body. The third sub-stages extended from 18 to 20 years. Both men and women were given compulsory military education at this stage.

The higher stage of education lasted from 20 to 35 years. At 20 years, there was to be a test and those showing aptitude for science and philosophy were given further education for 15 years. Here again, it was divided into two sub-stages, the first extending from 20 to 30 years and the second stage from 30 to 35 years. During the first stage, subjects like Mathematic, Astronomy, Logic, and other sciences, etc. were taught. At the age of 30, a selection test is conducted. Only those, who qualified, were given a further training for five years. During this stage, emphasis was to be laid on dialectics because according to Plato, dialectic was the only system of knowledge through which the highest reality could be achieved. This stage of education is for the creation of philosopher king. The philosopher king is expected to rule up to 50 years, and to retire and resume study for the contemplation of God.

Prof. Vicki and the Greek philosopher, Plato have shown us how important is curriculum and syllabus for imparting education to the student. Let us reflect on some of their thoughts and study the syllabus system that we have in Manipur.

1. According to the National Policy of Language in Education, it is a three-tier system, namely: 1. English, 2. Hindi, 3. Mother tongue. But the big question for the tribals is which dialect or language should be treated as the mother tongue? Certainly not Meteilon because they are not Meitei. Then, why is Meiteilon (Meitei Mayak) made a compulsory language up to class VIII in the valley for the tribals? This leads to studying another language, which then becomes a four-tier language system (including Meiteilon and the mother tongue of the tribals), which is against the National Policy of Language in Education.

2. Education through syllabus is the easiest and the most effective way of imparting alien culture to the indigenous people. I have gone through my daughter's class VIII syllabus of the Board of Secondary Education of Manipur in 2012. Although she is a Tangkhul Naga, the mother tongue subject is Meitei Mayak, which is divided into two papers: (i) Manipuri Tengpang Sahitaya, where the syllabus comprises mainly casual stories, taken from the dominant valley ethnic group. (ii) The other paper (Text book) is known as Manipuri Sahatiya. The contents of the syllabus are mainly of Meitei ethos and culture, a lesson like: (1) Meitei Haona Lonzat amasung mingkao, (2) Sumang leela, (3) Poets of Meitei, (4) Kang sanaba (indigenous games of Meitei), and (5) Nar Singh, etc., thereby forgetting and ignoring the tribals or hill people's ethos and rich cultural heritage, where its population is 33.43 per cent (as per 1991 Census Table 3.5) and its land consists of 91.75 per cent (Horam, R., 2014: 5) of the entire state of Manipur.

In the fifth semester syllabus of the three years degree course (B.A.) of the Manipur University, last year one subject known as "Northeast Development" was introduced. It was made common and compulsory subject for both Arts and Science students of the fifth semester. It has five units and one of the unit's topic is about "Manipuri Women". It deals in length about Nupilan (women war), Maira Paipi

(Women torchbearer), etc. It further explains in detail the role of Meira Paipi, which act as vigilante for warding off anti-social elements, drunkards, etc. to have peace. But it totally ignored the best example of peace making practice by Tangkhul women during the time of war, which is known as "Pukhreila" (Shimray, R., 1985: 168-169). The power, function, and role-play by Pukhreila of the Tangkhul women for peace making is unique and the greatest act, which is surprisingly missing in the topic of Manipur women and peacemaking.

Manipur State consists of multi-ethnic languages and religious groups. Therefore, it is sensitive in all aspects. Ignoring, underestimating or imposing other language and culture will be detrimental to peaceful coexistence, because every ethnic and religious group would like to preserve its own identity.

3. The National Policy of Education has made it a law not to carry heavy bag in school beyond the child's body weight proportion, as this may affect his/her health. As per the syllabus of CBSE and other central Boards, the contents of the books are usually brief and short to the point. Hence, the books are usually thin. However, the books of the Board of Secondary Education of Manipur are unnecessarily lengthy, books are usually bulky, and the syllabus is tough and not written direct to the point. They also have two textbooks for each subject, known as textbook and supplementary working textbook. This leads to heavy load of bag, which is hard to carry by the tender young students.

4. Plato's suggestion of curriculum of education – music for the development of soul and gymnastic for the development of the body is very important, the Manipur Board curriculum lack such things.

5. 21st century is a century of Information and Technology revolution. Today an educated person without computer knowledge is considered as illiterate. The Manipur Board must make a syllabus that can make all the students computer literate.

6. As we have rich cultural heritage, some of the important custom, culture, Indigenous knowledge like nature or plant medicine, treatment, environment, manner and other traditional culture and customary laws of the tribals, etc. should be included in the syllabus so that our children can be aware of our social, cultural and political heritage too.

7. A farsighted plan, vision, consistence and systematic framing of syllabus is needed, so that student may not have any confusion.

8. In order to have equal right in education, imposing only certain ethnic group's culture and dominant attitude in making syllabus must be avoided.

9. Language is one of the most important and sensitive issue in the education system. Moreover, a state like Manipur, which is composed of multi ethnic communities, it becomes more serious. As much as valley people would like to preserve their language, the other tribals also would like to preserve and study in their own dialect; after all it is their mother tongue. The tribal people feel that instead of developing the tribal language in the hills, Meiteilon is imposed on them. This is revealed in the memorandum submitted to His Excellency, The President of India by Tribal Students Union, Manipur on 14th July 1999, in point two, which mentions about the imposition of Manipuri language, "There was no education among the tribals before the advent of the British. It was only they, who introduced and brought education among the tribals. From that time onwards English was learnt. We had never learnt Manipuri, we do not learn it now, and we are not going to learn it in the near future also. For the three languages, the formula will become a four-language formula, which is an extra burden for the tribals and must be removed permanently. After a gap of century, the state of Manipur has been trying to impose their language on the tribals through educational institutions and competitive examinations. The recent imposition of the major Indian language (Manipuri) as a compulsory paper 1 in the All India Civil Services Competitive Examinations from 1998 for the candidates of Manipur, including the tribals candidates, has shocked all sections of the tribals. We shall never compromise on this matter. We are very apprehensive for the future of the tribals more than ever before. The latest imposition of Manipuri language on the tribals is in the Elementary School Leaving Certificate Examination at class VIII level, which no tribal pupil will be able to pass. Vide Government order of 16th January, 1999, no Language can be imposed upon the tribals, now, nor in the future."

In the executive summary of the National Curriculum Framework of 2005, it was suggested that "In language a renewed attempt to implement the three-language formula is suggested, along with an emphasis on the recognition of a child's mother tongue, including tribal language, as the best medium of education."

The latest language imbroglio is about the scrapping away of Additional English from the curriculum of class IX starting from next academic session (2014-15). Additional English subject was created mainly for the tribals, whose mother tongue is not yet recognized by the government or for those tribal students in the city or town, where there is no class or facility to learn their language in spite of being recognized by the government. The present curriculum of BSEM comprised five subjects, namely First Language (MIL) or three other subjects (Elementary Manipuri, Elementary Hindi, and Additional English); English, Mathematics; Science and Social Science. After removing Additional English from the First Language (MIL), Elementary Manipuri and Elementary Hindi, however, would remain. Languages included in the MIL are Manipuri, Hindi, Assamese, Bengali, Nepali, Sanskrit, Tangkhul, Thadou-Kuki, Mizo, Zou, Mao and Rongmei. Scraping Additional English means that the tribals, whose mother tongue is not yet recognized by the government or tribals, whose mother language is recognized, but do not have the facility to study their mother language subject in a school where he/she is studying, have to opt Meiteilon (Meitei Mayak) or Hindi, which is nothing less than imposition.

Education System in Manipur

Manipur State is a land of mysteries and turmoil. Its diverse social composition of multi-ethnic, multi-language and multi-religion made it more complicated, leading to political unrest, cultural upheaval, and economic stagnation that grapples the education system. Slowly and steadily, there emerges economic social class, creating economic disparity, which further leads to inequality of education development. This further infuses the conflict between elite and the uneducated layman.

On the other hand, the dominant ethnic group in the valley takes the advantage of the poor and helpless condition of the innocent villagers, hence, the disparity and the gap between the rich and poor and educated and uneducated becomes wider.

Some of the issues that affect the Education System of Manipur are:

Manipur state is fluid and fragile. It is sensitive in all issues, it is because multi ethnic and multi religion people reside in this tiny state. As the Government cannot appease all, there is always discontentment in one way or the other, therefore there is frequent bandhs and blockages, which badly affects the education system.

Manipur state is one of the most corrupt states in India. Often the best and committed teachers are not recruited due to corruption; hence, the result is not a desirable one.

There is rampant practice of proxy teachers in the schools of Manipur, particularly in the hilly areas. This is because the teachers do not have interest in teaching, or the posting area is too remote as the government has not adequately developed it, or the lack of basic health care and communication, etc. forced them to look for alternative means. Surprisingly the Government of Manipur is not serious enough to tackle this illegal practice.

Manipur is a home for many ethnic communities. Therefore, it faces the problem of which language to consider as the mother tongue; which language to learn and which to ignore. This is one of the serious issues, which provokes other communities repeatedly. Moreover, there is identity crises, which affects the education system in Manipur.

Manipur State is not economically sound. Most of the people live from hand to mouth. Hence, due to economic constraints, the education of their children cannot move forward smoothly.

The Government of Manipur does not have a transfer policy, hence, all the teachers try to stick to their most convenient place by hook or by crock, leading to bribe and corruption. Moreover, the deserving teacher is not given promotion or service incentives, etc., hence, the teachers lose job motivation, which adversely affects the education system.

There is frequent interference from the politicians with regard to transfer, promotion, administration, development, etc. These greatly hamper the system. In Manipur, such practice is common.

The student career and studies are in stake if the teacher, who should be the role model for the student, is not a committed one. Committed teachers in Manipur are not plentiful.

It is said that the curriculum is the roadmap for the students. Unplanned and unjust syllabus and curriculum will lead to nowhere. It is an irony to see that in Manipur some dominant ethnic group tries to manipulate, ignoring others. This can lead to disintegration in the end and affect the harmony and peaceful coexistence.

Education, educating students is always a teamwork. Parents, teachers and students have an equal role to play, only then it can bear fruit. Ironically, motivation and the role to be played by the parents are lacking behind in Manipur, particularly, the tribals parents send out their children to town and cities and never care to monitor and motivate them. Hence, they become like a ship without a rudder.

Learning through formal education should be made enjoyable to the learner. This can be done through various creative ways and means. Because of forcing the student to learn, trying to press down knowledge from outside in the form of listening or too much taxing the student may result in the student losing interest in studies. Such system is mainly in practise and prevails in most of the schools in Manipur. Learning through creativity needs to be encouraged, so that the students enjoy as well as the knowledge grows from inside. This reminds me of Plato's statement, "The elements of institution should be presented to the mind in childhood, but not with any compulsion; for a freeman should be a freeman too in the acquisition of knowledge. Knowledge, which is acquired under compulsion, has no hold on the mind. Therefore, do not use compulsion, but let early education be rather a sort of amusement; this will better enable you to find out the natural bend on the child" (Plato, p. 536).

Education is the root of our life. The present turmoil, social unrest, economic stagnation, etc. can be rooted out with proper education. Plato said, "Virtue is knowledge." If it is so, then only proper education can give knowledge and the proper education can be acquired only through proper syllabus. Hence, making proper syllabus and curriculum is the need of the hour to have good education, so that through proper education, peace, justice and development can be restored in this fragmented and turmoil ridden state of Manipur.

References

1. Arora N.D.: McGraw Hill. Delhi. 2012.
2. Board of Secondary Education of Manipur–BOSEM–BSEM.
3. Curriculum and Syllabus for Board of Secondary Education of Manipur.
4. Das. P.G.: New Central Book Agency, London. 2013.
5. Horam. R.: Sunmark Publisher and Distributors Delhi. 2014.
6. National Curriculum Framework 2005. NCERT.
7. Plato: Book VII.
8. Rao Venkata V.: S. Chand & Company Ltd. Delhi. 2002.
9. Dr. Vicky Casella.: http://www.psu.edu/celt/PST/syllaabus.html.
10. Shimray, R.R.: New Delhi, 1984.
11. Sabine H. George, Thorson L. Thomas: Oxford & IBH Publication Co. Delhi. 1973.

7

Tangkhul-Naga Grammar

A Study of Word Formation

Victor Ahum

The Problem: General Assumptions about Morphology

We begin this introduction by the question 'Where's morphology?' and we would find a variety of answers running from 'just in the lexicon', through 'in the lexicon and the syntax', to 'everywhere'. At various times, linguists have wondered that one of the key unresolved question in morphology is 'What is a word?' We can view the various answers to the question, 'What's morphology?' as implying answers to the question 'What is word?' And the answer to that question turns out to have different answers at different levels of representation.

Thus, there are conflicting criteria for word-hood. Language consists of words. Such is the verdict of folk linguistics everywhere. Languages generally have an expression that means something like the English term 'word'. The range of meaning of the expression varies from language to language, often extending to quite large stretches of speech, but the notion of 'words' in the sense of the units of language that are listed in the dictionary, is widespread, quite possibly universal, in human speech communities. Many linguistics have assumed that the 'word' in this sense is, in fact, a universal unit of language, definable within an accepted body of linguistic theory, and at various times in the history of linguistics, serious attempts have been made to formulate such a definition.

During the period of American Structuralism, however, the word was de-emphasized as a linguistic unit in favour of the morpheme. The chief reasons for this de-emphasis were two: the structural and functional diversity of the word across languages and the general unstructured nature of the lexicon in comparison with grammar and phonology. Much attention was lavished on morpheme, which, as the minimum unit of meaning or the minimum unit of grammatical structure, was by definition universal, whereas the role of the word varied so much from one language to another that it was conceivable that in some languages, the word could be almost or fully identical either with the morpheme or with the sentence. For instance, let us examine the following 'two-word' sentences in Tangkhul-Naga:

i m∂̀-và-kùi-z∂̀t-p∂m-η∂nào-nái-k∂̀c∂̀η-kh∂̀t-m∂-n∂̀

I NEG-go-round-walk-sit-play-want-real-INTSF-IND-COP, which may be translated something like:

> 'I seriously don't want to go and keep on going/walking round and round just for fun'

Such a sentence in Tangkhul-Naga would seem strange, if not nonsense, to, say, an English speaker that the two-word sentence is to be translated into English in so many words. (Again, there is not always word-for-word or morpheme-for-morpheme correspondence between the source language and its translation). But such constructions are very common and quite natural to the speakers of Tangkhul-Naga (and other agglutinative languages). In the same way, the speakers of Tangkhul-Naga might consider the so-many-worded English translation as something strange or unnatural.

Studies of the 'word' as a 'minimal free form', the 'formative' (which was the successor to the morpheme), and the question of the phonological characteristics of lexical representation or the place(s) in the grammar where lexical insertion takes place, the semantic structure of words in connection with the elaboration of semantic theory, and even lexicography as the study of the properties of words and relations among them, all did not pay much attention to the morphemic structure of words. Many morphological theories/models have been advanced, but there are more conflicting criteria for wordhood.

Morphology and the Lexicon

Morphology is in the Lexicon

Word forms or phrases that do not conform to rules of form or interpretation must be memorized by the native speakers and, therefore, listed in the lexicon. By that notion, then, the lexicon is the repository for the idiosyncratic. But that is not what everyone means by the lexicon. For some, it is also the word formation component, on a par with any other component. Many continue to distinguish the dynamic lexicon as word formation component from the permanent/ static lexicon, which is not only the list for the idiosyncratic, but also the register of all existing words.

Listing whole words would account for the inheritance of irregularity by a derivative or inflectional element. An exclusively morpheme-based theory that does not recognize words stored in the lexicon has difficulty accounting for inheritance. And, there have been no good arguments against the listing of all derived categories, for example, ci 'that' as a determiner, pronoun, quotative/ complementizing verb, etc., this is not an insurmountable problem. One could invoke Walinska de Hackbeil's 'Root Identity' principle [(1986: 34)[1] : "If a Root Rj is listed in the Root Lexicon with a set L of lexical properties, it may not be listed with a set M, and L ≠ M"] to prevent the listing of derived categories. However, it is not clear that this is either necessary or desirable. Nevertheless, we can assume that: (a) the output of productive word formation is subject to listing, and (b) productive word formation is a constant source of new lexically listed words. I will continue to assume, then, a lexicon of roots (word, stems and affixes) and words.

A root can have a representation on many planes. For instance, an affix may have no phonological form on the segmental plane, but may be linked to a tonal slot or timing slot on the skeletal core, in which case, it is realized as tonal rising and vowel lengthening. Thus, consider the following examples:

(1) à–ca – kúm 'last year'
(2) à - cá - kúm 'the year before last year' (tonal rising)
(3) à - cá: -kúm 'many years ago' (vowel lengthening)

This approach substantially unifies 'concatenative' and 'non-concatenative' morphology.

We can now present a unit-size hierarchy, which corresponds to a hierarchy of listedness as under: Listedness hierarchy

(All) morphemes (affixes, roots and underived stems/word bases)
(Most) derived stems
(Many) derived words
(A number of) compounds
(Some) phrases
(A few) sentences

Linguistic units in the above presented hierarchy increase in compositionality from top to bottom. A hierarchy of this type determines the degree to which derivatives can be made, that is, fewest based on frozen sentences, more based on phrases, and so on. It is also generally accepted that in agglutinative languages, like Tangkhul-Naga, where words are more phrase-like or sentence-like, derived words have a higher degree of compositionality, requiring fewer of them to be listed.

Lexicalist and Syntactic Theories of Morphology

The place of word formation has been the subject of much debate since the late 1950s. Early transformational grammarians continued the structuralist tradition of blurring the morphology/syntax division.

Chomsky (1970) saw an opposition between the 'trransformationalist view' and the 'lexicalist view', which transferred to the lexicon proper the rules of derivation compounding. In the lexicalist view, the rules of word formation are rules for generating words, which may be stored in the dictionary. Halle (1973) sees the dictionary as a set of morphemes plus a set of word formation mechanisms: word formation occurs entirely within the lexicon. The growing importance of the lexicon and the debate on the state of word formation meant the steady reemergence of morphology as a separate area of study. In the 1970s and 1980s, important works on morphology have been produced within the generative framework.

Recently, interest has grown in natural morphology and in lexical phonology and morphology, 'Lexical Phonology' for short. Natural morphology is an approach which looks for natural universals over a wide range of languages with regard to 'morphotactic' (the way morphemes are joined) and morphosyntactic tendencies. Lexical phonology regards the lexicon as the central component of grammar, which contains rules of word formation and phonology as well as the idiosyncratic properties of words and morphemes. The word formation rules of the morphology are paired with phonological rules at various levels or 'strata', and the output of each set of word formation rules is submitted to the phonological rules on the same stratum to produce a word. The lexicon is, therefore, the output of the morphological and phonological rules of different starta put together.

Most recently, we have seen a bumper crop of new books on the foundations of morphological theory. Among the leading theorists are: Spencer (1991), McCarthy (1992), Matthews (1991) and Lieber (1992).

Spencer (1991) is an admirable comprehensive overview of research in generative morphology. He elucidates the special theoretical problems posed by nonconcatenative phenomena (for example, Semitic root-and-pattern morphology, reduplication, and morphophonemic solutions that have been proposed for them. Such solutions have the paradoxical effect of bringing what seemed to be indisputable instance of processual morphology into the purview of morpheme-based conception of word structure. Spencer also provides an illuminating overview of the problems, which clitics pose for any delineation of the boundaries among syntax, morphology structure and phonological. He examines mismatches between morphological structure and phonological or semantic structure. For Spencer, the only successful account of the full range of such mismatches will be one that countenances a paradigmatic dimension of word formation. Spencer concludes with the assumption that morphology is an autonomous component. Synthesizing several independent lines of reasoning, he proposes a composite model in which rules and principles of morphology function as well-formedness conditions applicable at more than one level of representation – that is, applying not only to lexical representations, but in at least some instances to syntactically or phonologically derived objects as well. The idea is an intriguing one, but the details (particularly concerning the limits intercomponent interactions) remain to be worked out.

McCarthy (1992) distinguishes five focal issues, which Chomsky and Halle (in the late 60s and early 70s) brought to the fore: (1) the contents of the lexicon, (2) productivity and semantic regularity in word formation, (3) the internal structure of words, (4) allomorphic variation, and (5) the inflection/derivation distinction, and surveys the range of opinions, which generative morphologies have subsequently taken on these issues. McCarthy examines recent investigations of the relation between morphological form and meaning. His approach is that of 'Natural Morphology' whose principles of 'naturalness' which, through the possible mediation of typological or system-specific factors, mold a language's morphology.

What morphology can contribute to general linguistic theory? McCarthy concludes that, in their eagerness to reduce morphological principles to independently needed principles of phonology or syntax, 'mainstream' generative morphologists have ignored those aspects of morphological structure having no ready analogue in the domain of syntax and phonology. Particularly glaring, here, are the lack of a consistent approach to allomorphy and the nearly total neglect of the lexical-semantic dimension of linguistic structure. McCarthy is optimistic about the possibility of uncovering morphological principles of Universal Grammar; but because the 'poverty of stimulus' argument is less obviously applicable in the domain of morphology, he warns that morphologists cannot follow syntacticians in pursuing the 'single-language approach' to the discovery of universals –'that in morphological theory-construction, there is no alternative to detailed comparison of a wide variety of languages'.

Matthews (1991) distinguishes three logically separate notions of 'word' – word, word-form and lexeme. This affords a clear conceptual distinction among inflection, derivation, and compounding. Matthews distinguishes the various senses in which 'morpheme' has come to be used and explains the kinds of morphological systems that 'morpheme' and 'allomorph' are best suited for describing. He demonstrates that, the employing morphological metarules of a particular sort, it is possible to capture the same kinds of generalizations in a manner consistent with modern assumption. Perhaps such an idea will stimulate further inquiry into the structure of inflectional paradigms, heretofore an aspect of morphological organization too often dismissed as epiphenomenal. The validity of the traditional distinction between morphology and syntax is addressed where discussion inevitably centres on the notion 'word'. The various logically independent characteristics of words are examined, along with such complicating factors as clisis and periphrasis. Matthews also presents an enlightening account of the morphological manifestations of iconicity on both the syntagmatic and the paradigmatic dimensions. Works of the natural morphologists loom large here.

Lieber (1992) is an interesting and worth-discussing work. She claims that the rules of word formation are just the rules of syntax, but applied to sub-word units. The work surveys phenomena at the interface of morphology and syntax, showing how word formation or inflection can sometimes involve units larger than words.

Lieber argues that the principles of X-bar theory developed for syntax can be pressed into service for all productive word formations. This presupposes that words are comprised (exhaustively) of morphemes and that morphemes are lexical entries with subcategorization frames. Moreover, the head of a word is the derivational affix, which determines the syntactic category and other aspects of its structure. The base of affixation will then be a complement, a specifier, or a modifier. Ceteris paribus, the order of morphemes in word formation is identical to word order in syntax. Thus, in a language with SVO word order, a complement in, say, a deverbal compound will come after the stem, and in a SOV language, it will precede the verb stem. In a language with prehead modifiers or specifiers, derivation in which the base modifies or specifies the affix will be right-headed (i.e., suffixation), whereas in a language with post-modifiers or post-specifiers we will find prefixation. Lieber also surveys phenomena, such as circumfixing, conversion, apophony, reduplication, and root-and-pattern morphology, arguing that autosegmental phonology can handle most of these cases by reducing them to 'Item-and-Arrangement' morphology.

Lieber's work represents an ambitious attempt to reduce morphology to syntax and phonology. For many readers, this may be seen as the death-knell of autonomous morphology. Here, we might feel justified in asking how the 'morphology-is-syntax' proposal would deal with straight-forward cases of, say, derivation and agglutination in Tangkhul-Naga, which exhibit more interface between morphology and other components of grammar than between morphology and syntax, and word formation rules often going directly counter to syntactic structure. In many languages, there are pronominal affixes, which cross-reference subjects and objects. Often their order correlates with basic syntactic order, but not always.

I would argue for essentially the opposite of Lieber's approach. Morphologists have no reason to fear imminent redundancy and replacement by syntacticians. Morphologist should establish domain-specific principles and, on the basis of these, determine how morphology interfaces with other grammatical components. After all, if we don't look for specifically morphological principles and they happen to be there, we will never find them.

To sum up, the models of morphology that have emerged over the recent years illustrate that much of the intellectual challenge posed by morphology for the linguistic theory-construction lies in the exploration of the interface between morphology and the rest of the grammar. Age-old questions concerning the nature of words are given novel interpretations, while at the same time, new phenomena are unearthed, which may well have gone unnoticed under the older perspective. This is precisely what we want of a vigorous and developing brand of study.

Scope and Orientation of the Study

This research, more importantly, is about to bring Tangkhul Naga word formation into the mainstream of linguistic discussion – documenting the various word formation processes. Since no scientific or exhaustive research has been done in this language in any area, let alone word formation, I have to employ my own expertise relying much on the large-but-not-so-coherent works on word formation in other languages. It is my hope that this research will help redefine the notions, such as 'word', 'phonological word', 'morpheme', 'formative', and so on.

This research is concerned with word formation in an 'independent model' (a synthesis of models, in other words).

I have not strictly followed any particular morphological theory or model. This is partly because, at the moment, the study of word formation is in a state of flux, and there is no one body of accepted doctrine on the subject, so that, often researchers are compelled to make up their own theory and procedures as they go along. And, as the present study is more or less exploratory in nature, I have more or less followed a 'morpheme-based descriptive' model of word formation with an attempt to list all the affixes (derivational and inflectional) and as many morphemes as possible in compounding and reduplication. In part, the decision not to strictly follow any particular model or theory has been motivated by my personal interests. Another reason for such decision is that Tangkhul-Naga is an agglutinative tone language in which various typical structures and word forms are widespread, and no single theory or model advanced so far is capable of accounting for all the numerous peculiar features. One could hardly imagine, for instance, the existence of structures in Tangkhul-Naga, such as compounding of two plural markers with two classifiers in a single 'word'; 'concrete nouns' taking the nominalizer or formative affix, and so on.

A variety of specialists have interest in word formation and I hope that this research will prove useful to the phonologists, systacticians, historical linguists, descriptive linguists, and others whose main interest lie outside morphological theory as such. In addition, phsycholinguists and computer scientists working on language processing would find that this research relates to their concerns. Finally, it is my hope that this research covers many key theoretical issues confronting contemporary linguists with an interest in word formation.

The Place of Tangkhul-Naga in the Tibeto-Burman Family of Languages

The language of the present study is simply known by the ethnic name 'Tangkhul-Naga'. 'Tangkhul', phonemically/taçkhul/, belongs to the Naga sub-group of the Tibeto-Burman family of language.

Dr. Grierson (1903), in the Report of the Linguistic Survey of India, assigned each of the Naga language a definite place in the family of Tibeto-Burman languages. According to him, between Angami-Naga and the Bodo languages, there is a group, which he calls the Naga-Bodo group, bridging over the difference between the characteristic features of the two forms of speech, and similarly, between Angami-Naga and the Kuki languages, there is another group, which he calls the Naga-Kuki group.

The Naga-Bodo group, according to Grierson, consists of two main languages, viz., Mikir… and Kachcha Naga… Subordinate languages closely akin to, but not dialects of Kachcha Naga, are Kabui Naga and Khoirao Naga… As might be expected, the Bodo languages with which they show the most important points of kinship is the eastern one, Chutiya; while Angami and Lhota are the two Naga tongues to which they are most closely allied. It must, however, be confessed that with regard to Kabui and Khorao, the classification is somewhat arbitrary, for, though they have undoubted connection with the Bodo languages, they also show many points of contact with Kuki ones… The Naga-Kuki subgroup includes Sopvoma or Mao-Naga, Maram, Miyangkhang, Kwoireng or Liyang, Luhupa or Luppa language, viz., Tangkhul and Maring. The language of the Mao Naga most nearly approaches the true Naga languages. Of these, it possesses the closest resemblance to Kezhama… Indeed, Sopvoma is so closely connected with all the languages of the Western sub-group (in which are included Angami, Sema, Rengma and Kezhama) that it might with equal propriety be classed as belonging to it as to the Naga-Kuki one. These three languages (Sopvoma, Tangkhul and Maring) exhibit a regular gradation in the change of speech. Sopvoma is most nearly connected with the Western Naga languages, and Maring with the Kuki one, while Tangkhul occupies an intermediate position.

Thus, according to Grierson, we have languages connected with typical Naga dialects, with Kuki elements, the influence of which gradually diminishes as we recede from the area occupied by kuki tribes. We have language related in part to Bodo dialects, in part to Naga dialects, while containing Kuki elements. Grierson's classification is claimed to be based on morphological analysis. However, we find his classification rather arbitrary and superficial.

His use of the term 'the true Naga languages' is also not clear. In fact, there are some non-Naga tribes included in the Naga group (for whatever reason), and their difference is quite evident not only from their customs, but also from their languages (especially in morphological structures).

A.E. Gait (1906), in "History of Assam", states that 'with the exception of Khasi, the numerous non-Aryan dialects of Assam, all belong to the Tibeto-Chinese and mainly to its Tibeto-Burman sub-family. The dialects of this sub-family, which are current in Assam, belong, in the main, to three groups, viz. Naga spoken in and east of the Naga Hills; Kuki-Chin spoken in Manipur, Cachar and the Lushai Hills.

Konow (1909), in "The Tibeto-Burman Family", made a more comprehensive study of the sub-family and finds the Naga languages as a distinct group having not much connections, as Grierson claims, with the Bodo and Kuki-Chin languages.

Geographical and Demographic Distribution

Tangkhul-Naga is spoken by all the Tangkhuls numbering about 15,00,009. The Tangkhuls occupy the entire Ukhrul district of Manipur – a hilly terrain spreading over 1823 sq. miles and the adjacent borderline of Myanmar. There are some 220 Tangkhul villages and about 20 Kuki villages in Ukhrul district.

Ukhrul district is bounded in the north by the Mao hills of Manipur and Nagaland (inhabited by the speakers of Paumei, Mao, Maram, Angami, Chakheshang, etc.); in the west and south-west by the Sadar hills and Imphal valley of Manipur (inhabited by the speakers of Mao, Paumei, Thangal, Maram, and Mitei); in the south by the Imphal valley and Chandel district (inhabited by the speakers of Mitei, Andro, Makeng, Maring, Anal, Chiru Kom, Paite, Thadou, Lamkang, and Mayon-Monsang); and in the east by the Kabo valley of Myanmar (Burma) (inhabited by the speakers of Burmese Kuki, Kachin, Somra, Haimi, Hlangan, Rangpan, and Tsaplaw).

About 20 per cent of the Tangkhul population are scattered outside Ukhrul district, in the surrounding areas in Manipur, Nagaland and north-west Burma. Sizable portion of Tangkhul speakers is found in

Kohima and Dimapur valley in Nagaland. Important 'colonies' with major Tangkhul concentration in Imphal–the capital of Manipur State – are Tangkhul Avenue, Nagaram, Dewlaland, Mantri Pukhri, Chingmeirong and Checkon.

Tangkhul is the second largest Naga tribe, next to Konyak tribe of Nagaland and Myanmar, in terms of number of speakers. There are some 40 Naga tribes, which are spread over:

(1) the entire state of Nagaland;
(2) the Ukhrul district, Senapati district, Chandel district, Tengnoupal district, Tamenglong District, and Sadar Hills of Manipur;
(3) the states of Assam, Tripura, and Arunachal Pradesh;
(4) the Kabo valley and along the Indo-Myanmar border in Myanmar; and
(5) the southernmost part of Yunan Province of China.

An Overview of Grammatical Studies on Tangkhul-Naga

The Tibeto-Burman sub-family of languages (to which Tangkhul-Naga belongs) is of considerable interest to the linguists and cultural historians of the Himalayas and has been the subject of large, but mostly unproven hypothesis. Till the 1940s, the great majority of the Tibeto-Burmic-Naga languages were unwritten. Many of them are spoken in regions difficult to access.

We do not have evidence to prove that Tangkhul-Naga was ever widely employed till the early 20th century. Today's standardized Tangkhul came into existence only at the close of the 19th century with the arrival of the Britishers. The Britishers set up their administrative headquarters at Ukhrul village and created the Ukhrul sub-division comprising of nearly all the Tangkhul villages. The administrators and the missionaries, then, had chosen the dialect of Ukhrul village for compiling, writing and translation of short vocabularies, biblical books and school texts, and, in due course, made it the standard or common language of all the Tangkhuls. Today, the Tangkhul lexicon is comprised of various village dialects in which the Ukhrul dialect occupies the largest portion.

The study of Tangkhul-Naga was initiated by Rev. Fr. N. Brown in 1837 with the publication of three short vocabularies entitled 'North

Tangkhul', 'Central Tangkhul' and 'South Tangkhul'. For decades and decades, most of the lexical surveys, grammatical notations and elementary books were compiled by missionaries aiming at or helping ecclesiastic newcomers to start more easily with their jobs, and above all, to provide Holy Scriptures to new converts. In 1918, Rev. Fr. W. Pettigrew brought about the Tangkhul-Naga Grammar and Dictionary.

Some of the recent worth-mentioning works on Tangkhul-Naga are: D.N.S. Bhat (1969), 'Tangkhul-Naga Vocabulary', James A. Mattisoff (1972), 'Review of Tangkhul-Naga Vocabulary'; S. Arokianathan (1980) Tangkhul-Naga Phonetic Reader and (1987) Tangkhul-Naga Grammar.

Though these pioneering works are of much value, they are not linguistically sophisticated. For instance, Arokianathan's short discussion is, if not a distorted one, full of discrepancies. His analysis is, perhaps, based on wrong data and information.

So Broken a Linguistic Landscape: Multilingualism

Apart from the 'common' or 'standardized' language, the Tangkhuls speak various dialects – each village has its own dialect named after the village. The fragmentation of the linguistic situation among the Tangkhul-Nagas is so deep that nobody can really say how many inter-village dialects are there (according to my estimation, there are more than 150 inter village dialects). The intelligibility among the village dialects varies according to the distance between them. Farther the village, the more is the unintelligibility.

Although the concentration of the Tangkhul-Nagas in the entire Ukhrul district was more, each village was on "head-hunting" war with the other. Constant attacks from the neighboring villages made their life uncertain and let them to seclusion. This seclusion, I think, is the main reason for the gradual development of the village dialects. Their conscious efforts for using and inventing secret codes due to fear of war with other villages added to the diversity, in due course, between the village dialects.

The Tangkhuls are bilingual in Mitei (or Manipuri) – the official language of Manipur State, and 'Nagamese' of 'Naga Pidgin', which is the lingua franca of Nagaland State. They communicate in Manipur with speakers of Mitei and other tribes in Mitei. They use 'Nagamese' or English in communicating with the speakers of various Naga tribes in Nagaland.

Inside the village, one interesting phenomenon is the use of both 'standardized' Tangkhul and the village dialect interchangeably in various contexts. Before the advent of the 'standard' Tangkhul, speakers of the neighboring villages communicated with one another using each own's dialect. And till today, we find many elderly people doing the same. Such type of communication is dying out with the younger generation. Inside the village, people use only standard Tangkhul in the Church – to read the Bible and sing hymnals in standard Tangkhul. It is also the medium of instruction in schools. However, both the standard and village dialect are used, as the occasion demands, in both formal and informal speeches – in meetings, festivals, entertainments, and so on. Surprisingly, all 'prayers', be it of an individual, a family, or larger groups, are said in standard Tangkhul. In other words, every Tangkhul speaker, who can speak standard Tangkhul, prays to God in standard Tangkhul.

Methodology

Since Tangkhul-Naga is my mother tongue, I have primarily utilized my native speaker's intuitions. In other words, this research employs 'First Language' approach or mentalist approach and inductive methodology – trying to account for the native speaker-hearer's competence. The source of data is the contemporary forms of usage of the language as is reflected in the literary works and formal and informal speeches. Data have been collected and cross-checked as much as possible from informants through questionnaires interviews and observations. My judgments are verified, not only with the village dialects of Tangkhul-Naga, but also with other Naga and Kuki-Chin languages. In essence, I have approached various theories and models as the research demands.

Notes

1. H.W. de Hackbeil (1986), The Roots of Phrase Structure: The syntactic basis of English morphology. Cited in D.G. Miller (1993), Complex Verb Formation. p. 3.

8

Social Enquiry of Educational Scenario

The Mapithel (Pesii) Range of Ukhrul District, Manipur

Mes Jajo, Lucy Jajo and *Maheishang Awungshi*

The centrality of education – and of public involvement in education – in any society can hardly be over-emphasised. This is particularly true of our place in the society, and the welfare of the society is dependent upon education. In short, education is essential for all for an all-round development, material and spiritual and, hence, its importance in shaping towards a progressing future is of eminent importance. There is need to redefine education in the tribal belt of Manipur in general and Ukhrul District in particular.

This article attempts to inquire, and analyse the prevailing educational system in the Mapithel Range of Ukhrul District, Manipur. It evaluates critically the various problems besetting these areas and tries to come forward with some constructive findings and suggestions that can be both qualitative and quantifiable in theory and practice.

Education has continued to evolve and diversify its coverage since the dawn of history and every country develops its system of education based on its unique socio-cultural identity to meet the challenges of the time. The National Policy of 1986[1] is one such significant step in the history of education in post independence India. Recent years have seen certain important committees and commissions deliberate on education. In order to bring about quality education, 'The National Curriculum Framework, 2005' proposed radical shifts in theory and practice of schooling. It redefined knowledge and expanded the sites of learning. It explicitly proposed a paradigm shift from 'objectivism' to 'constructivism'. Further, the document perceived the child as the 'constructor of knowledge', hence, accordingly, it viewed schooling from a 'process' perspective. As regards the notion and definition of literacy and illiteracy, there have been at least three different standpoints in India from three different agencies, viz.: (i) Census Department; (ii) educationists and planners and administrators of formal education system; and (iii) those dealing with adult education/ literacy. National Knowledge Commission (2006) Report on higher education supports a strong reform agenda through public investment. In line with the goal of nation building, India has been committed to providing free and compulsory education to all children. Towards this end, Indian Parliament has enacted a legislation known as the "Right to Education Act, 2009", it becomes imperative that compulsory and free education be provided to children aged 6-14 years for the completion of elementary schooling, which has come into force from 1st April, 2010. Rashtriya Madhyamik Shiksha Abhiyan (RAMSA) has been launched recently as a step to universalize secondary education. However, there is a huge challenge in terms of ensuring the provision of a democratic, inclusive, high quality and creative education system. These challenges are the more significant because the legitimate aspirations of most of the tribal population, which has hitherto been effectively excluded from access to quality education, can no longer be ignored. The challenges can be summarised briefly in terms of: the need to ensure adequate public funding for all levels of education, which have so far been hugely underfunded; the need to ensure access to quality education, which is neglected.

Mapithel or "Pesii"[2] is a small hill located in the south eastern part of Ukhrul District of Manipur, which also forms a great wall of hill range for the Imphal valley. It is inhabited by nine (9) small villages namely: Lungphu, Shinta, Marau, Shingkap, Tangkhul Hundung Khullen, Tangkhul Hundung Khunao (Greatland), Itham, Zingshao, and Bohoram, and is popularly known as the Zingsho Mapithel Range, with a total house-holds of 824 (eight hundred twenty four) and population of 3360 approximate. It is connected to Imphal city by deplorable/dilapidated road condition. The inhabitants of these ranges (tribal population), hitherto has been effectively excluded from access to quality education. Quality has both absolute and relative meanings. The concept of absoluteness in quality props up the moral of the education system at the delivery end and at the receiving end, i.e., Institutional and Students, respectively.

Table 8.1 gives a general view of the prevailing condition of educational system in this Range. In all the schools mentioned above, Shingkap High School is one of the oldest High School in the area. It was established in the year 1935 as JP School, which was upgraded to a full-fledged High School in the year 1972. Shingkap Government High School acted as the centre of learning for the past many years and had produced 80 per cent of total matriculates in the area. In 2013, the total number of student enrolled was 75 as against 120 in 2012. There's a decline of 45 students. Tangkhul Hundung Khullen, and Lunghu are the two newly upgraded Government high schools with a total of 44 and 139 student enrolments against 50 and 129 in 2012, respectively. There is a decline of six in the case of Tangkhul hundung Junior High school. However, a slight increase of 19 pupils in the case of Lungphu High School. Shingta Primary School has 75 enrolled and the actual number of pupils attending the school is 39, as against 81 in 2012. The actual number of enrolment in Marau Primary School could not be obtained, however, from the information gathered, only 31 students were actually attending the school. In Tangkhul Hundung Khunao Primary School 35 student were actually attending regular classes, Bohoram has 24 students enrolled, but only 12 students are attending the school; Itham 21, actual 4; Zingshaou has 25 students in 2013 as against 30 enrolled in 2012, but none were actually attending the school. All the villages in this range have access to schools, some primary and some high schools. However, it should be noted that access to schooling facilities is not an indication/ indicator of quality infrastructure and quality education. This also need not guarantee that children of different age groups are benefitted.

To analyse the stated problems, we break up the staff into teaching and non teaching staff as shown in the Table 8.2. Lungphu Government high school has only three Arts graduates, no Science Graduate teacher and no Headmaster. There is a huge human resource deficit: – there is shortage of science teachers; language teachers – Hindi, Manipuri, Mil; physical instructor, clerk and chowkidar. The villager has appointed additional 12 teachers to meet the need. It charges an admission fee of Rs. 800 despite the fact that RTE prohibits charging of fees, as per the provision clearly stated for free and

Table 8.1

Name of Village	*Total + Population*	*No. of Households*	*Presently Residing*	*Types of School*	*Staff*	*Student Enrolment*	*Actual students*
Lungphu	800	148	120	High School	10	139	139
Singta	380	50	40	Primary (ADC)	8	75	39
Maraou	600	105	70	Primary	6	—*	31
Shingkap	900	168	120	High School	7	—*	75
Great Land	180	47	28	Primary	2	—*	35
Tangkhul Hundung	800	196	176	Jr. High School	6	44	44
Bohoram	150	45	26	EGS (ADC)	1	24	12
Itham	95	45	18	SV/Primary	7	21	4
Zingsou	52	17	10	Primary	2	25	nil

Table 8.2

Village	Staff										
	Teaching					Non Teaching					
	Arts Grd	Sc. Grd	Hindi	Man	Un Grd	Mat	Clrk	Peon	Cwk	Cook	total
Lungphu	3		nil	nil				1		4	8
Shinta	6					2					8
Maraou	4					2					6
Shingkap	1	3	nil	nil	2	1	nil	1	1	3	12
T. Hundung kl	1	1	nil	nil	2	2					6
T. Hundung kn			2								2
Zingshao					1					1	2
Ithum	7										7
Bohoram	1										2

Source: From field work.

* The enrolment of the student could not be obtained as the headmaster was absent at the time of investigation. Here, the total population is derived from the currently resident house-holds excluding those house-holds that have migrated to towns for works-related and educational purposes.

compulsory education. Nevertheless, fee is charged to pay the salary of the village appointed teachers, borne by the village council and the church. Shingta Primary School has six graduates, two matriculate teachers; the school is functioning under the Autonomous District Council (ADC). The case in Marou Primary School is more or less the same. It has four graduate and two matriculate teaching staff with no clerk, peon and cook. Shingkap Government High School, despite being the oldest school in the area, has only seven teaching staff and five non teaching staff out of the total sanctioned post of 21 (teaching and non teaching staff, without cook). To fill the gap, the VEC/SMDC, in consultation with the school authority, has appointed another five teachers, and one volunteer under ECCE is also utilised in the school. The situation in Tangkhul Hundung Khunoa Primary School is grimmer; it has only two teachers, out of which one has been utilised as the CRP of Shinkap Cluster under SSA. The lone teacher has to take care of the students enrolled in different classes, so, it does little justice to the students. Tangkhul Hundung Kl. Jr. High School has 44 students enrolled in different classes, with only six teaching staffs: one graduate Arts and Sciences, two undergraduates and two matriculates. Bohoram EGS School has only one teaching staff, as the EGS School is defunct. In view of the needs and necessity of the children to pursue education within the village, the village authority, in consultation with the parents, agreed to keep the appointed EGS teacher and also engaged another teacher to teach the children. And for that purpose, the students were charged an admission fee of Rs. 50/- per student and monthly fees of Rs. 200/- per student. Also an amount of Rs. 1000/- per month is being paid by the Village Authority. Zingshao has one teaching staff and one non-teaching staff, Itham village has SV and Primary School has a total of seven teaching staff.

In all the schools mentioned, there is an acute shortage of teaching and non teaching staff. Regarding this unequal rationalization of teaching staff in the tribal and non tribal areas, the Naga Youth Front in 2010 carried out an investigation in which the report states, "Many teachers under the Education Department are given to Meities for hill areas and almost 100 per cent of them have been transferred to the valley with some excuses, thereby leaving behind just 3-4 teachers in all schools."[3] Similar views were pointed out by the president of the All Tribal Students' Union, Manipur (ATSUM), parents and tribal teachers from all the nine schools seem to strike in one accord that "In the valley, teachers are in excess and most of the teachers from the valley, who are posted in the valley, got themselves transferred either with post or without post to the choice of their location on the pretext of their security reasons."[4] Coupled with this problem of human resource deficits, there is high prevalence of teachers' absenteeism and the practice of employing 'proxy teachers'[5] by the government employed teachers irrespective of the hill-valley divide (tribals and non-tribals alike).

There is poor infrastructure and all the schools do not have the basic necessities, for example, there is no toilet, no drinking water facility, no lab, or library facilities in Lungphu Government High School. The old school building is being used as hostel and teachers' quarters for students and teachers, respectively. Though there is provision for the distribution of free textbooks uniforms, bags and incentives, The textbooks supplied were insufficient, with no complete set as required by the syllabus and only a notebook each was given to the students. The school received uniforms for 139 students attending the school. No facilities were provided for Children With Special Needs (CWSN) in spite of the fact that there is a 12 year old, who is paralyzed from waist down below. The plight of the school in terms of infrastructural deficit is briefly highlighted below:

Case I. Singta Primary School

1. No MDM kitchen.
2. No library.
3. No drinking water facilities.
4. The floor of the classrooms were broken and uneven.
5. There is no proper partition between the classrooms.
6. Most of the school's windows and doors are broken.

Case II. Marou Primary School

1. ACR under construction.
2. Inadequate desks and benches.
3. SGT under construction.

4. Insufficient classrooms as three rooms are used as chapel hall.
5. No MDM kitchen.

Case III. Shingkap High School

1. No MDM kitchen No separate toilets for boys and girls.
2. There is one common toilet constructed under RMSA. No drinking water and library facilities.
3. Some of the classrooms have broken floor. The school teacher quarter is in need of major repairing.

Case IV. Tangkhul Hundung Khunao

No School toilet. No Mid Day Meal Kitchen. Insufficient classrooms. No drinking water facility. No library.

Case V. Tangkhul Hundung Khullen

1. School class-room extension (three rooms): As the implementing agency of the work had put up only the foundation and left, the villagers have boarded up the walls, partitions, windows, doors, etc. And the rooms are being used as class-rooms.
2. School building old and battered.
3. Classrooms insufficient.
4. No toilet of any kind.

The prevailing education system gathered from the field indicates their common grievance, that is, the government apathy to their plight – in adequate teaching staff. In most of the case, the schools observed in all the villages were almost in defunct conditions. The school buildings were quite degraded and there were only a few students, and none in some cases. There were no single toilets for the students, no drinking water facilities in all the schools that were visited. The quality of furniture, such as benches desk, blackboard in many of the schools are below standard. The villagers in all the villages have only little or no hope in the government schools. Moreover, they were a little apprehensive about the visit as most of the visits and promises made by various educational departments were not fruitful. Despite various schemes and programmes for the universalization of education, envisioned goals of strengthening the two ends of the spectrum, namely, elementary education and higher/technical education would help in meeting the objectives of expansion, inclusion and excellence in education. The state has failed to deliver all the goods, i.e., quality education at both the delivery and receiving ends.

There is a huge challenge in terms of ensuring the provision of a democratic, inclusive, high quality and creative education system. These challenges are more significant because the legitimate aspirations of most of the tribal population, whose living conditions were poor, sending children to other places for pursuing studies adds more burden to them. Education has been politicized deliberately by the dominant groups against the less privileged minority. Thus, there is a huge gap, the valley areas are maximally developed, whereas the hill areas are lagging behind by minimal educational development. Therefore, the provision of ensuring a democratic, inclusive quality education, which has hitherto been effectively excluded from access to quality education, can no longer be ignored. There is the need to ensure adequate public funding for all levels of education, which have so far been hugely underfunded; the need to ensure access to quality education, which is neglected. In order to improve the quality of education in the area, the government should provide all the infrastructural needs of the educational institutes of the area. There should be a proper rationalization of teachers. It will be also useful on the part of the intellectuals to mobilise the community about modernising trends of education in which the government adopts different policies to improve the quality of education. Above all, sincerity and honesty among people for the betterment of the future society will do a great job. This can happen if the education system is made creative throughout and full employment opportunity is provided to all; then only the education system can retain the smiles of children and fulfil the mission of education in Dr. Kalam's words, "It (education) is the foundation to ensure the creation of enlightened citizens, who will make a prosperous, happy and strong nation".

Notes and References

1. It aims to promote national progress, a sense of common citizenship and culture, and to strengthen the national integration. It also laid stress on the need for a radical reconstruction of education system to improve its quality at all stages, giving much attention to science and technology and moral values and a closer relation between education and the life of the people.
2. Pesii is a local indigenous term that the people used to identify themselves before they were corrupted to Mapithel by the Maharaj of Manipur during the colonial period.
3. Webcasted on 02 June 2010, at www.nagalimvoice.com
4. *Security Reasons* here cited has a deeper connotation; it may be either real or imaginary/fictive. In an ethnically divided society like Manipur, where there is a covert conflict between the tribes and non tribes, it becomes a convenient tool.
5. Proxy teacher here refers to the illegal practice of subletting others by the government employed teachers as substitute on their behalf by paying a mere sum of money. According to a survey by NGOs, like VVD and PASDO, this is practiced in 83 per cent of the villages in Ukhrul district.

9

Education and Spirituality in the Present Context

R. Wonkhuimi

"Educators are healers, who trust in the wholeness of life and of people". – Dr. Rachel Naomi Brown

Education is called *Vidya* in Sanskrit. It is derived from the root word *Vid*, which means 'to know'. The term education has its origin in Latin word 'educare' which means to 'elicit'. Education is an activity or a process, which transforms the behaviour of a person from instinctive behaviour of a person to human behaviour. There are two aspects of educare, the worldly and spiritual. Worldly education brings out the latent knowledge pertaining to the physical world. And spiritual education brings out the inherent divinity in man. Man, instead of acting impulsively, acts rationally. In order to make him act rationally, spirituality is an essential aspect of education, but it hardly finds place in the present system of education. The worldly education relates to the head and is ephemeral. Reading, writing eking out livelihood and attaining name and fame, all these result from worldly education. The worldly education makes man great, whereas spiritual education makes a man good. The spiritual education relates to the heart, compassion, truth, forbearance, love and forgiveness. "Spirituality means the state of being marked or characterized by the highest qualities of the human mind, through the creative, animating power or divine influence of God." Webster Dictionary.

In a technology driven world today, where there seems to be shortcuts and cheat codes to everything, spirituality has most definitely taken a backseat. Life is about practicality and achieving what has not been achieved. In order to do that, people can go to any level of standard, moral degradation and even to the extent of murder, because people are driven with the selfish motive of achieving more and more. Everybody seems to be in a hurry to earn a living that is of the highest standard and more. Emotion is no longer a word or expression that is respectable any longer. Man has become more or less like a machine. It is because the educational system totally ignored the spiritual aspect. We can also say that the present system of education is lopsided giving more importance to cognative and ignoring conative and affective side. That's where we have gone wrong. We have the best educational system today that specializes in teaching our children on how to become the greatest of scientists, doctors, accountants and so on and so forth, yet there is this great sense of emptiness that has most definitely taken over most of them today. The spiritual poverty of contemporary education provides few opportunities for today's youth to quench their deep thirst for meaning and wholeness.

Imporatnce of Spirituality in Education

There have been educational institutions for centuries. What started as an unconventional way of teaching young ones the basic activity to hunt and eat have now evolved to a state where there are schools to teach and guide the children to prepare them to be self-sufficient adults. Proper educational institutions come from religious milieu. Be it Christianity, Hinduism, Islam, or Buddhism, all major religions had institutions to guide both the children and the adults to cope and learn to live the right way. From the Ten Commandments of the Holly Bible that is given to the Christians, such as Honour thy God; Honour thy father and thy mother; Thou shalt not kill; Thou shalt not steal; Thou shalt not commit adultery; Thou shalt not bear false witness against thy neighbor; and Thou shalt not covet thy neighbour. These are some of the golden texts of the Bible. Likewise, the Dharma of the Buddhists and the Hindus teaches the simple truth of non-violence, love and forgiveness. The tenets of Islam are Honour God, Honour Parents, etc. In order to maintain relationship with God, one has to pray to God at least five times a day.

For what worth is it to study the ecosystem and not love your neighbour? Or to know how to operate on a heart and have no compassion? The education system today has taken a life form of its own. Every country has its own way of teaching and generating teachers, who can bring out changes and different means and ways of enhancing education. There is competition amongst institutions to outdo the other. This is the primary source of education and this is where the race begins. Children are pushed to think out of the box. The crazier the invention, the more famous you can be. One cannot deny the wonders this is doing for the world today, yes, but again what are we doing to balance this immense stress? Physical and mental well-being must be balanced for if a man has physical health, but no mental stability, he is on the way to becoming both physically and mentally sick and vice-versa. Yet, there is no dearth to the different types of institutions cropping up in every nook and corner of the world to take care of anything and everything one can only imagine to face. However, there is no denying the sterility of it all. The emptiness is palpable and almost life-like. Most people today are cold and ruthless, not to forget selfish and lost. They know what they want and they almost seem mechanized to achieve it no matter what the circumstances. One cannot deny, something is definitely amiss, that is the need of spirituality in education. Today, the students have no trace of value in them.

Need of Spirituality in Education

Our education system today seems flawless. No matter what part of the world we are, we are all well aware of the history and lifestyle of those living many oceans away. We know why there are natural calamities and have discovered cures to diseases that have killed millions. In the eyes of a technology-crazed world, everything is perfect. But if asked why there are so many young students committing suicide and killings in the institutions, especially in elementary schools, we can understand that something has deeply gone wrong. Everything is being taught to perfection what the students need to know of the plants, the planets, the animals and the whole world and the complexities of the whole system. On the other hand, misguided or unconscious attempts by students to attain some sense of fulfillment often result in varying degrees of addiction behaviour toward activities, substances or relationships all of which make teaching and learning difficult, if not impossible. Compulsive or reckless activity, substance abuse, and empty relationship can result from students trying to escape the pain of an inner emptiness. In the classroom, this can manifest as lack of interest, lack of self-worth, lack of compassion, lack of self-discipline and lack of spirit. We can come to just as many solutions, but we must also agree that an earlier intervention by giving importance to spirituality in education would have most definitely helped. The alarming rise in the number of AIDS patients and the more alarming fact that the youth and younger generation are the one most affected is not lost on the world. Frustrations and the want for a fast life despite knowing the risks involved are driving many today to the brinks they can no longer control. Today many young people are like beautiful cars without brakes. Without moral and spiritual development, the young people are left nowhere.

Spiritual and moral education should be included in the curriculum. The Chavan Committee Report (1999) submitted to Indian Parliament emphasized the need to nurture core universal values like truth, peace, love, righteous conduct, and non-violence in students. The National Curriculum Framework for School Education (2000) echoed the sentiments expressed in the earlier policies regarding erosion of social, moral and spiritual values and suggested the integration of values in the curriculum. The National Curriculum Framework (NCF) 2005 has recommended an integrated approach for education for peace incorporating the entire school life-curriculum, co-curriculum, classroom environment, school management, teacher-pupil and parent-teacher relationships, teaching-learning process, and the entire range of school activities. Education for moral value cannot be done by the school all by itself, as it is a shared responsibility of the other stakeholders too.

Below here is a compilation of teachings from some of the major religions that can be applied in today's educational curriculum, since all religions have virtues.

1. *Christianity*: The 10 Commandments, The Golden Laws of the Bible (Exo. 20: 3-17).
2. *Hinduism*: "If filled with egoism, you think, 'I shall not fight,'

your resolve will be in vain; your own material nature will compel you (Bhagvat Gita 18:59).

3. *Buddhism*: Suffering is caused by craving (The Four Noble Truths, Point).
4. *Jainism*: The Triple Gem of Jainism – Right vision or view (Samyak Darshana), Right knowledge (Samyak Gyana) and Right conduct (Samyak Charitra).

These are just varied examples of teachings from these religions that can be implemented worldwide. Inculcating them with the present curriculum, students not only learn from the books, but also give them a more insightful understanding. A more 'soulful' education seeks to open the mind, warm the heart and awaken the spirit of the student. It would provide opportunities for students to be creative, contemplative and imaginative. It allows time to tell old and new stories of heroes, ideas and transformation. It encourages students to go deep into themselves, into nature and into human affairs. It values service to others and the planet, a planet that is going through her most turbulent phase. Learning to love nature opens the door for the children and young adults to respect and keep their own environment clean and taken care of. Teaching to respect one's elders will help them in their dealing with future relations, as they attain positions where they will be dealing with respective countries and all the unfathomable heights, they will achieve.

The Role of Teacher

A teacher is anyone, who helps others learn to behave in new and different ways. This could include anyone from parents to drill sergeants. Teachers are supposed to teach what is 'good', good is a value laden concept. Sometimes the idea of good may differ from one to another. Even though it is difficult to have universal concept about what is good teaching, the good teacher is one who is able to bring about intended learning outcomes and imbibe the spirit of Truth, which is the fear of God. Without objective, students' behaviour becomes random and unpredictable. If the students do not actually achieve the learning goals, the teacher cannot truly be called an effective teacher or a good teacher. An effective teacher is the one, who had received a sound education, that is, all round development spiritually, intellectually, physically and emotionally.

Mc Kinney (1987) identifies five elements of effective instruction, which can be applied in teaching in all types of education.

1. Good teachers set clear goals and stick to them. Without focused goals, students may learn about many topics, but master none. Good teacher can accomplish two or more goals simultaneously.
2. Good teachers carefully communicate expectations. They explain what students will be studying and how it can be useful. Good teachers connect new lessons to past ones and show how they relate to everyday life. They monitor students' work carefully to ensure accuracy and completion and teach strategies for learning in and out of the learning environment.
3. Good teachers thoroughly understand the subjects they teach. They also know the misconceptions students harbour and work to clarify and correct them.
4. Good teachers carefully select materials to fit in the curriculum and the characteristics of their students with the abundance of religious curricula available. Teachers generally should not have to create their own materials, although that may be desirable occasionally.
5. Good teachers believe that they are responsible for what is learned and how students behave, as opposed to those, who hold students totally responsible for their learning. Teachers, who assume that low-achieving students do little to encourage them to learn. Both teacher and student need to assess the situation and make necessary adjustments. The teacher is responsible for taking the initiative in this adjustment process.

An essential quality of a good teacher carries high sense of moral obligation. So, teachers have the moral obligation to see that their students live out to be outstanding citizens, who achieve not only in the eyes of the world, but also be fulfilled within themselves. They should be helped and encouraged and attain balance with their world at work, at home and be at peace with himself on the inside. Students must be fervently taught, the spiritual aspects of life. Teachers today must realize that this is not just for the students alone, but also an anchor cornerstone for them as well. There is pride in knowing that you have taught the book well, but there is greater pride in knowing that you have helped and guided an individual in becoming the best that he can be both in his professional and private life. Teachers should be living examples so as to encourage the young ones. Solon, the famous Athenian lawyer was asked near the end whether he gave his "best" laws. He denied and said that he gave them 'the best they were able to receive'. Teachers must learn to be as Solon, not only giving the best they can, but also the best the students can receive.

Everyone has been put on earth for a purpose. Some are called to be healers, some are to be leaders, some to be builders and so on and so forth. But what all of these have in common is that they have had teachers, who taught them and inspired them in becoming citizens with ideal principles. The passion to teach and nurture the young is indeed a gift that cannot be taken for granted. Just as the potter moulds his clay to be perfect and impeccable, so must a teacher mould the students to be the best they can achieve inside out.

We live in a conceited world today and as teachers, we must be all the more vigilant so as not to fall prey to, because we have seen through history and even today as to how much damage corrupt leaders can bring about. Our moral duty to teach the students the right path of life through spirituality must come with self practice and discipline. We cannot further ignore the glaring desolation that has gripped the world today.

Conclusion

True spiritual education can only transform a person's life into a state of being in the highest qualities of human mind. Implementing spirituality in education can bring forth a surge in the traits and characteristics, like:

1. Love, compassion and service.
2. Truthfulness and honesty.
3. Responsibility and discipline.
4. Tolerance and patience.
5. Faith, trust, and inner security.

6. Divine wisdom and understanding.
7. Inner peace and joy.
8. Physical, emotional, mental and spiritual clarity.

References

1. Tanija V.R. *Educational Thought and Practice.*
2. *Handbook of Children's Religious Education*, Religious Education Press Birmingham, Alabama.
3. Rise Richardson talk on Spirituality and Education Italy, January 2010.
4. Holistic Education Tasmania: July 97 News.
5. Jahnabi Baruah, Research Scholar, Assam University Silchar, Spiritual and Moral values in Education and Curriculum: A point of view. A seminar paper.
6. McKinney, K. (1987). *Five tips to improve teaching*. Research in brief. Office of Educational Research and Improvement. Washington, DC: U.S. Department of Education.

10

Women Education and its Potential of Harnessing Sustainable Handloom Industry in Northeast

Lucy Jajo Shimray

Modern educators regard education as a process that should be relevant to the situation, looks for innovative changes out of the present dilemmas. Modification takes place indirectly through the use of knowledge in its various forms that can be communicated by educator (Bhatia, 2000). The sociological aspects of education defined education in the stimulation of child's power by the demands of the social situations in which he finds himself. Thus education involves the interplay of the educator, educand and the social forces where the educator tries to modify the personality of the educand in the light of the needs and demands of society to which the latter belongs. (Dewey, 2000). In this backdrop, it is important that women who have been playing crucial role in traditional Tangkhul economy, in handloom sector in particular, need to be imparted with new innovative ideas through education in order to sustain and improve their efficiency. This will result to enhancement the scope for sustainability of handloom industry and will continue to provide various socio-economic benefits to almost all the community in the form of weavers, buyers and market products. The inherent knowledge of women weavers and the rich culture of diversity can be showcase through the handloom products both at the national and international level. This will further expand the scope of economic venues such as employment generation and thus open up ways of income earning opportunities and social services towards the concerned host communities. Hence, educating the women weavers can shed the light of the presently existing potential and exhibits their personality and talents through various products which speaks volume about the culture, tradition and ethnicity.

Handloom sector today is emerging as one of the most income earning profession in India. With the 'Incredible India' campaign India has now attracted the attention Worldwide as a fast emerging country in terms of economic growth and its development. Since 1990, Indian government's agenda of 'Look East Policy' particularly for the Northeast region, the region has been increasingly in the nation's socio-economic focus. Now recently with the bilateral Free Trade Agreement (FTA) between India and Myanmar and opening up of Trans-nation highways through Manipur via Moreh, it has become pertinent and an issue of debate as to how far Manipur can benefit from this Trade relations. At this particular juncture, one of the new factors influencing the NE areas has been development of handloom sector as one potential product having large avenues of export promotion as it is the second largest industry only next to agriculture. At this backdrop women in NE region can play a significant role for the sustainability of their livelihood through promotion and production of handloom sector in the border trade policy between India and Myanmar.

Handloom sector plays a very important role in the country's economy. It is the largest economic activity after agriculture providing direct as well as indirect employment to more than 30 lakhs of weavers (Soundarapandian, M., 2002) in the country. The government therefore is making exploring the possibility of making optimal use of the resources. With almost one fourth of the total textile production and contributing substantially to the export earnings, the handloom remains dominant industrial segment of the country. In fact, many countries benefit from handloom as part of economic development factor. Historians considered India as the birth place of cotton manufacturer recorded to have originated during the Vedic period. In most of the states in the region, handloom is regarded as a rich village industry which in most case is a hereditary occupation. The significant of handloom industry in India was clearly found in the description contain in the writings of a Chinese traveller of the 13th century (Soundarapandian, 2002) where it narrates that every household used to prepare cloth to be self-sufficient in clothing. Handloom was treated as cottage industry and a family occupation. Even the best fabrics were made with the help of rudimentary tools by people in their own home. India ranks third in the world in terms of cotton production accounting to 5 per cent of the world production.

Handloom industry in Manipur state has an unrivalled craftsmanship and is spread throughout the length and breadth of the state forming as part of socio-cultural tradition of the people having rich cultural heritage. The National handloom census of 1995-96 reported Manipur as having 4.62 lakh handloom workers which is second in position among the top states of the country having 2.81 lakh looms (manipurhandloom.com; 2011). Almost unlike other states, Manipur handloom weavers are all women. Thus it is obvious that women has a lot of scope for enhancing her skill and improve her socio-economic status in the society but unfortunately, till today her status remains inferior to her male counterparts in many aspects. She could not produced the required amount of handloom products as demanded in the market due to so many constraints that will be studied in the following paragraphs

Keeping in mind the above statement of introduction, the main objectives of the present paper is given as follows:

(i) To study and identify the various prospects of handloom products in Manipur and Ukhrul.
(ii) To highlights the role of women as potential handloom producer and also to promote as sustainable livelihoods and social security especially for women in the large scale.
(iii) To study the various aspects of problems and constraints faced in the due process of the production.
(iv) To suggests strategies for improvement of women in Ukhrul and Manipur as handloom producing destination in tune with the Look East Policy towards planning and policy frame work.

Historical Background of Handloom in Manipur/Ukhrul

Manipur state with her comfortable climate and mystic cultural heritage and vast unexplored natural resources promises to be a huge potential for growth of handloom industry in future. By its physical feature, Manipur is a hilly land locked state with a small valley constituting only 1,843 sq.km out of the total 22,237 sq.km. It is surrounded by hill ranges on all sides accounting more than 90 per cent of the total geographical area. The state is inhabited by the major group Meitei along with other 36 ethnic indigenous groups of people and Meitei-Pangal respectively (Lucy Jajo & Binota, 2012). Since time immemorial, Manipur is known to the outside states for her artistic excellent handloom products. Handloom weaving is thus treated as a respectable profession in every home in Manipur. Every women irrespective of caste, creed, and rank is born a weaver. In fact no mother could think of giving her daughter away in marriage unless she becomes an expert in weaving. From time immemorial handloom in Manipur has been known for her beauty, distinctive feature of colour consideration, excellence in design and textures with different traditional designs. Historical records reveals that loin-loom weaving was practised in Manipur before the birth of Christ as far back as 87 A.D. (Singha & Sharma, 2005).

Before the introduction of mill made cloth in the state, weavers produced all cloths necessary for human consumption. Cotton was grown abundantly in the hills dyeing was done with indigenous things with of different colours produced from the Earth, flower, hearth, bark and seed of fruits but gradually declined with the introduction of mill cloth. Once which was indigenous industry has now depended totally on raw materials in the form of yarn outside the state. In 1910, Mr. Pillary from Bengal was engaged where he brought Automatic handloom to trained Manipuri weavers but could not progressed well and a new fly shuttle loom was brought in 1920 from Serampore by a local Meitei and flourished well in the state (Singha, 2005). While fly shuttle looms are found more in valley, loin-looms are still dominating in the hill areas even today. Nonetheless, the native weavers are still continuing extensively with the loin-loom. Handloom weaving of loin-loom form a part of the socio-cultural tradition of the people of Manipur and Ukhrul in particular which has rich cultural heritage.

Ukhrul district is dominated by Tangkhul Naga tribe mostly Christians, speaking Tibeto-Burman language of the Mongoloid origins (Yumnam, 2011). It is considered as the highest hill station in Manipur away from capital city Imphal by 83 kms in the East district out of the existing five hill districts collectively. Majority of the people depends on agriculture as their sole livelihood. Of course now with the initiatives of some NGOs horticulture plantation are being taken up on large scale. The average literacy rate in Ukhrul constitutes 81.7 per cent with 86.5 per cent males and 77.4 per cent of females respectively (Lucy Jajo & Binota, 2012). However, due to unemployment among the educated youths, people mostly women considered handloom as the next best alternative for their livelihood. Most of the weaving is done in a loin-loom or back strap. The traditional skill of handloom weaving is not only a status symbol for the womenfolk but it is an indispensable aspect of socio-economic life. Further promotion and up gradation of handloom in Ukhrul district can be identified as thrust key area of interest due to its unrealized potential and further promote as an alternative for sustainability in the region. As it is, sustainability is gradually becoming part of mainstream agenda and gaining a momentum globally.

Status of Women in Ukhrul District

As mentioned earlier the Tangkhul women are the backbone of the society in terms of socio-economic development. The contribution of women in weaving is their artistic art of weaving beautiful designs of indigenous cloths which is an inborn quality and a traditional profession since time immemorial. It largely substantiates their economic condition in supplementing the family income. This is often showcased to outside tourists through cultural festivals and fairs and thus contributing a lot for the economic welfare of her family and even for the society at times. Right from the kitchen table to schooling of children and agricultural practices the work is not complete without women's participation. Moreover women are now holding high government posts in varying capacities. But this does not guarantee a respectable status for women in all domestics and community affairs. Women still faces the brunt of structural biasness though in different forms. (Eyingbeni Humtsoe, 2010). Taking these into account, handloom products of women in Ukhrul and Manipur can be initiated as essential item of commodity to be exported in varying degrees and earn a name as destination of traditional handloom products in the national and international arena. This will give a sense of social security and economic independence to the women while at the same time pave the way for inclusion in public discourse in dealing with social issues at varying levels.

Since time immemorial women in the Tangkhul society are regarded as peace maker and her voice is equally respected by all men specially in times of war and conflicts in the form of 'Pukreila' (it means peace maker) despite the fact that the society follows patriarchal type of social system. Due to gradual improvement of educated women, the voice of women in any platform is well acknowledged by their male counterparts. In fact the children have more attachment to their mothers than their fathers. This in itself speaks volume about the role women has in the family household too. Consequently, conscious efforts are on the move to include women in the public discourse of dealing with social issues for more accommodative and positive signs of progress that are deemed quite appreciable by the society. Today we have many lady Doctors and well qualified Academicians and social activists to name some few. According to the 2011 census the literacy rate of Ukhrul district in Manipur constitute 81.35 per cent as against 85.52 per cent male and 76.95 per cent female. The total literates constitutes altogether in Ukhrul district alone accounts 129,829 people (female literates constitutes 59,681 and male constitutes 70,148 persons).

Source: Economic Statistics of Ukhrul district 2014.

In the present context we now find many Tangkhul women holding high posts and offices in both private and public sectors. In fact we have the first Lady MP (member of parliament) Mrs. Shiningla Keishing in Manipur from the Tangkhul society to cite an example. Many Tangkhul women are now holding high government posts in many Departments and high religious positions. Hopefully with more genuine and sincere support from all sides women can take equal share in contributing to social transformation and nation building. Here the quotation given by Prof. Haimendorf is worth mentioning: "*Many women in more civilized parts in India may well envy the women of Naga Hills, their high status and their free happy life and if you measure the cultural level of a people by the social position and personal freedom of its women you will think twice before looking down on the Nagas as savages*" (Horam, 1977), this clearly depicts the unique culture of the Nagas and more particularly the Tangkhul

Naga women who enjoy utmost respect and regards in the midst of the patriarchal system.

Many Tangkhul women today are actively involved in social movements under various women frontal organisations such as Naga Mother's Association (NMA), Naga Women's Union Manipur (NWUM) taking the lead and playing a pivotal role in mitigating the impact of violence and conflicts in the Region. As such women can organise fairs and festivals in Ukhrul district head-quarter by inviting tourists and visitors both domestic and outside tourist to take part in the festivals and occasions and showcase their unique culture, arts and crafts and traditions through their handloom products. This can help built cohesive relations between communities in the state and between countries at large. Braving the modern sophisticated weapons even of the arm forces women are ceaselessly volunteering for peace and social justice with the militants and the security forces for social security and emerging as the front line against any rights violation. Redefining education in the hill districts of Manipur calls for such initiatives and promotion so that it can ensure accessibility, profitability and sustainable development in the region in the long run. It needs commitment, sincere genuine interventions. Handloom sector can serve as the platform for women's emancipation of empowerment socially, economically and politically.

Importance of Handloom

Manipur in general being disconnected with the rest of the world in most cases due to geographical location is still industrially backward. The living standard in both hills and valleys is quite low as compared with their mainstream. Due to lack of basic infrastructural facilities, the regions' rich natural resources and forests resources specifically remain unutilised. Therefore, though the region is an agro based economy, weaving is regarded as one of the important household industries which occupies a prominent place in the economy of the state and hills particularly. Moreover weaving is a part of their culture, a way of life with them and the absence of this skill is considered uneducated and unbecoming in their modern traditional set of beliefs. Thus, weaving is considered as an art of basic cultural inborn gift and talent which passes down from generation to generation. It is one quality of every women in the society. Handloom is treated as an indispensable aspect of socio-economic life. Since agriculture and industry has not really taken off in spite of the potential which remains still unexploited, the pressure for employment is on the service sector and handloom sector mainly for women. As it is, handloom is a rich village cottage industry. By and large, at present there are about 5,00,000 people or 21 per cent of the total population absorbed as either full time or part time weavers. About 80 per cent of the women are engaged in producing handloom cloths providing as the largest scope for earning to womenfolk. The sound of the handloom is the music of every rural home in India. The handloom weavers achieve harmony of motion and rhythm. Basically there are three types of weavers in Manipur viz.:

- Individual weavers,
- Master weavers, and
- Weavers under cooperatives societies.

The kind of loin-loom used by the women in Ukhrul is popularly known as 'Primitive loom'. The primitive loom though outmodeled have remain unchanged for generations because of its simple structure easily usable by any weaver, the weft being threaded by hand for interlacing the warp ends. Though ancient and primitive in nature it is still capable of producing varieties of designs which is difficult to replicate even in the most modern looms. Thus it offers unlimited scope for indigenous designing. Another importance of handloom in Manipur is that there is a concomitant relationship between its origin as an industry and the cultural demand of society. It serves as a medium of transmitter of culture and civilization as there is the need of the costumes of different clans and various secular, religious occasions. According to the Annual Administrative report, 2010-11, in Manipur alone there are 1700 handloom weavers' cooperative societies with 1,89,465 members respectively. (Kshetrimayum, Otojit, 2011).

Prospects of Handloom Products

Each and every community has its own pattern of clothing in Manipur varying from one another. Each region of Manipur is specialised in the production of different traditional designs. Some of the most common products used by different groups are indicated below:

For Meiteis

The Meitei belongs to the majority group of people residing mostly in the valleys of Manipur state with various ethnic groups residing together since time immemorial. Mention may be made here some of the most common handloom cloths worn by them.

- *Moirangphee (Temple design):* It is a unique and important cloth used by the Meitei mainly the plain dwellers. Moirangphee has been derived from the place Moirang some 40kms South of Imphal. Its design is pyramidal in figures with geometrical and floral designs having one inch solid border. Its a beautiful design cloth quite commonly used by every member in the household.
- *Leirumphee:* This particular cloth is used on certain occasions and is regarded as an essential item for presentation during marriage ceremony. This Leirum itself has a lot of significance. When Pakhangba a Meitei warrior went to restore peace between the hills and the plains, people who were at war saw a Tangkhul women weaving a colourful cloth. She presented these clothes to King Pakhangba after which he named it as 'Leirum' in Meitei dialect and 'Ritamand' in Tangkhul dialect (Singh & Sharma, 2008). There is also a saying that in rituals of Meitei religious ceremony, a ritual is not complete without a Tangkhul cloth which relates the-inter bonding relation between Meitei and Tangkhul as brothers.
- *Likli design*: This is a famous cloth even used as dowry of a bride in Manipur designed and evolved out of a part of the loin loom called 'Thangu' a tool for processing and beating the handloom cloth. Examples of this cloths are bed cover, shoulder bag etc.
- *Shamilami design*: This cloth is typically designed and embroidered with Shamilami and animal motifs popularly known as Naga chadder. Legend of its origin dates back to

the Nagas that they used to cut out figures of animals from barks and leaves and stitch it on the shawl.

- *Phanek/Kashan*: This is the traditional dress of the Meitei women folk. Of course all the women in Manipur use 'Phanek' as lower garment printed in their own traditional designs and colours. This cloth is made out of cotton and silk with shades of various colours and is the most common handloom item which can be purchased both for personal use and trading purpose. 'Mayek Naibi' and 'Mapal Naibi' are famous designs of phaneks. Both the upper and lower areas of the phaneks are beautifully embroidered in about three to four inches, revealing a beautiful place of artistic skills of their traditional heritage and skills with the help of fine silk thread. This will have great economic benefits on the weavers in terms of their livelihood and social security.

Tangkhul Nagas

The Tangkhul Nagas inhabiting the Ukhrul district and regarded as the highest hill station in Manipur has more than 250 villages, speaks different languages of their own having some similarity with the adjoining villages. There are numerous designs of hand woven cloths, distinct and colourful as the main colours are dominated by red and black. Following are some of the common handloom cloths used in every occasion.

Haora and Chongkhom

This cloth is woven by loin-loom weavers. Earlier weavers used to weave in a single cotton yarn but in the present times almost all the cloths are woven in one ply of cotton yarn and two ply of woollen yarn. Whereas Chongkhom is usually worn by female in a three pieces with alternate black and red stripes in the middle. On the border is the design of motifs of spear designed in white and green. Haora is used and worn mainly by males in five pieces or seven pieces with the border design in motifs of spear with green and white or saffron colours. In all the festive occasions the people used to wear only traditionally woven beautiful attires which is quite fascinating and attractive at the same time. A single piece of this shawl cost not less than Rs. 2200 but the weavers could not weave more than two or three pieces at the most in a month.

Phangyaikashan

A traditional kind of *phanek/kashan* (wrapped around) used by the females. It is usually a three pieces cloth separately woven and join together. In the olden days this 'phanek' was meant for rich ladies only but now such restricts does not exist anymore and anybody can wear at her own choice and convenience. This particular phanek has a special significance. It represents goddess Phangyai, the goddess of wealth (Singh & Sharma, 2008). The symbol indicates a python possessing a very long hair and wherever it enters into anybody's field, it becomes a good omen of success. Besides this particular piece of phanek, there are numerous designs and colours beautifully designed and aristically created which attracts the onlookers wherever it is displayed in an exhibition or worn by the local women in any religious ceremony and cultural festivals and occasions. These are some of the unique indigenous products of Manipur handloom in general that will definitely attracts foreign tourists and investors for further trade relation between countries. In recent times professional weavers are weaving with thin silk with complicated beautiful designs and the price of this ranges from not less than 7,000 per kashan. The time duration taken to finish this cloth takes minimum three weeks to one month.

Thangangkashan

This is a special type of cloth to be used by the person who has proved his gallantry in war by killing enemies and having good house and having harvested a good amount of crops. In every household of the Tangkhul Naga society of Ukhrul district, the art of weaving is taken as a symbol of possessing feminine quality without which she is not respected by the older women in the strictest terms. As soon as a girl reach her puberty she is taught the art of weaving by the elder or her mother as a necessary requisites for attaining maturity and further specialised it for weaving different patterns as she desires. Thus it is an inherent trait. In recent years many designs and patterns are made out of this handloom or loin-loom cloth. Various handloom items from necktie, waist coat, and wallets to skirt, bags, purse, and chunis, the weavers weaved intricately in their own creative patterns and designs which are mostly envied when put on sale in exhibitions, fairs and festivals at the state level, and national level. These items are quite fascinating and attractive, In some cases curtains, carpets, doormats, cushion-cover, pillow covers are also beautifully woven from handloom. This is the line of departure where the present study mainly aims to emphasise on delivering the goods of handloom products further for promoting and sustaining the livelihood of women in Manipur and Ukhrul with proper marketing strategies so that in the long run it can compete at the national and international arena.

The Than-gang Kachon

This is a special type of cloth to be used by the person who has proved his gallantry in war by killing enemies and having good house and having a good amount of cup. In every household of the Tangkhul Naga society of Ukhrul district, the art of weaving is taken as a symbol of possessing feminine quality without which she is not respected by the older women the trust terms. Even a girl does not specialised in this art, yet, every girl bows the art of weaving as or inherent trait. In the recent years many designs and patterns are made out of this handloom cloth. Many handloom items of various colours are intricately designed quite fascinating and attractive. In some cases, carpet, curtains are also woven from the handloom weaving. This is the main objective of the study emphasised on delivering this goods of handloom products further for promoting and sustaining the livelihood of women in the national and international arena of marketing strategies. Besides there are still many types of meghala or kashan in varying patterns and designs woven by loin loom. Some other prominent type of kashan are: Seichangkashan (a three piece woven cloths use by female), kongrakashan (a two piece woven cloth with black and white stripe in the row in middle), Awungphilakashan, kamokashan etc. are some common items and popular among the Tangkhul women society. However, these products are sold mainly in the local market, in the form of primary products without any significant value-addition.

In addition to the above items, the Tangkhul women are now expertly producing some other form of handloom items with indigenous style blended with modern fabrics both for home consumption and marketing though not in a large scale. The unique traditional style of neck-tie, shoulder bag, waistcoat, skirt, purse, chunisetc are quite eye-catching to the onlookers. Notably maximum items of these products are being produced through the indigenous style of hand weaving (back-strap). If one would visit a Tangkhul Naga household personally, one would find a girl having done the morning chores, at the loom weaving even before going to the agricultural field or otherwise as her main profession of earning her livelihood. But unfortunately, due to financial constraint most of the weavers could not produced more than one piece within a time of two to three weeks. The weaving tools being obsolete and outdated women weavers could not procure modern tools and techniques which otherwise would make them economically more sound and stable. However, surprisingly it is worth the praise the amount of strength she endures to meet the ends need. Most of the weaving looms are primitive and indigenous in style. Just as the Kashmiri's handwork shawls and Lucknow chikkan are much more costlier than the industrial textiles so also the hand woven cloths of the Tangkhuls are much costlier than the one produced through power and fly shuttle looms. Women excelling in this field is something she must be proud of. A nature's gifted talent for which every woman in the Tangkhul society need to preserve with pride and dignity. A single piece of Meghala (wrapped around) cost not less than rupees two thousand. Women's potential of handloom weaving can be fully tapped and utilise on large scale for sustainability of their livelihood by expanding the horizon of marketing outside the state. Every mother should continue to uphold this culture by imparting the techniques of weaving to every girl child in the family irrespective of their status and class whether literate or illiterate. This can be one way of retaining the cultural identity, tradition and customs of the indigenous people in general. The prospects of women in the handloom sector can be fully developed and exposed in the national and international arena if necessary requisites be provided to her to fully explore her potential in this particular field.

Strategies for Handloom Promotion Towards 'Look East Policy'

As mentioned earlier, the thrust key area of this present study is to promote women through Handloom as sustainable livelihood and social security experience taking the advantage of the trade agreement between India and Myanmar with the vision of "Look East Policy" of the Indian government's agenda. Its is firmly believed that India's trade with Thailand could touch around US$ 7 billion by 2010-2011 due to propelling double transaction under Free Trade Agreement (FTA) (Chongloi, 2011). As business opportunities coexist with investment opportunities, collaborating Thai industries and Northeast entrepreneurs could give impetus to the lacklustre Look East Policy. Perhaps taking this advantage the women weavers of Manipur can robbed in themselves various in Handloom items as one essential item of excepts under FTA policy, so that Thailand's items of imports from India could easily include Handloom product besides other items already included. At present the Royal Thai Embassy is perhaps the only country in ASEAN region showing signs of interest in understanding the investment potential across Northeastern region of India especially in tourism, food processing and infrastructure. Manipur Handloom can even be introduce and promote as one potential tourism product in the state. Manipur has the advantage of acting as India's gateway to the rest through Moreh town, which is the only feasible land route for trade between India and Myanmar and other South East Asian countries. India's look East policy and several new measures taken up by the centre and the state government will certainly provide Manipur with a competitive advantage. Cleverly, the government of India has notified an integrated check post (ICP) at Moreh in recognition of the existing potential of Moreh, the border town of Manipur (Manipur, Chronicle, 2011). As the issue of globalisation takes place in the modern time, preservation of the few remaining cultural community around the world is becoming hard to challenge. In a backward region like Manipur and Ukhrul district in particular a tribal based community, having minimal negative impacts is an essential objective for reaching economic advancement to any destination planner. As such sustainable destination development of the area is vital in order to prevent the negative impacts of destroying the authentic identity of tribal community living in Ukhrul district.

Here in view of the present scenario, women weavers of Ukhrul district can take the challenge of showcasing their traditional handloom products in varying degrees of design and quality and try to make it to the front as an attractive Indigenous products attracting business interests and tourists. With the top business opportunities available in India for the 2010-2011 list which includes tourism as one of the sectors, handloom can be introduced in this tourism sector as one potential item of product included in Export-Import (EXIM) Policy strategies. Therefore, communities living in Manipur needs to re-align their strategies in order to reap the envisioned benefits. The people of Manipur in general should be ready for the great upheaval and changes in their lives and habitation by possessing the requisite trading, human capital and skills for reaping the benefits thereon, with the designated check post as notified by the India government. very items of products irrespective of cloths, industrial goods, consumers goods needed a good efficient channel of distribution. With a bold marketing strategy, the foundation for growth and success of handloom sector in Manipur and Ukhrul particularly can be laid down. Though not much progress has been made in business investment and various business opportunities since the First Northeast Business Summit in 2002 in the region, (Chongloi, 2011) its time the region do soul searching and root cause analysis so that the 'Look East Policy' turn into reality. With Tourism becoming a booming industry in India handloom has a lot of prospects to make it into the main business sector. Handloom being the largest industry in the state which has been flourishing despite many bottlenecks provides maximum employment particularly to the women. Keeping this in mind the state Government needs to concentrate in this particular sector seriously. Notably there are few handloom production activities being run by government machineries. They are:

(i) Manipur Development Society (MDS),
(ii) Manipur Handloom and Handicrafts Development Corporation (MHHDC),
(iii) Manipur State Handloom Weavers' Co-operative Society (MSHWCS).

Thus, Manipur has immense potential for business adventure in attracting potential investors. It only needs some effective implementation of the various policies and programmes as already envisaged in the governments' policy of National development.

Discussions

Knowing the fact that the main economy of the region is dependent on agriculture and other allied activities but due to under development of industry, there has not been much change in the main occupancy of the region in last decades. However, comparatively speaking, the valley areas are economically more developed than the hilly areas. Women's potential in handloom though it serves as major sources of livelihood, the weavers have not been able to produce handloom clothes with full potential owing to their economic backwardness in various steps for implementing various piglet and Schemes for improving handloom industry and the socio-economic condition of the weavers and still today it is lagging far behind the expectations. Due to economic constraints in terms of financial shortage, lack of proper training and design facilities, unavailability of raw materials at cheap rates and lack of proper marketing set ups has rendered most of the weavers way behind the mainstream. The economy of the region as a whole is still agrarian and its full potential is yet to be exploited. The resource rich state of Manipur generate very little in terms of economic produce. It has therefore become essential to expedite the full potentiality of handloom so that it can become a source for alternate livelihood for sustainability especially for women in Ukhrul district and the entire North Eastern Region in general. In the recent years few handloom exhibition has been promoted in Ukhrul district under the initiative of the state govt. and has proven to be quite successful. Such a move need to be expanded and organise frequently in order to let the weavers showcase their talent while reaping economic benefits at the same time. More societies, handloom industries should come forward to grant financial loans to the sincere and earnest weavers and self help groups or related societies. Except few weavers' societies and self help groups majority of the societies are defunct due to shortage of funds and raw materials. Eventually the potentials are not fully utilise and remain stagnant thereof. More so, too many leaders remain satisfied within the safety of male environments and continue to ignore the connection between the improvement debates and diversity.

Social insecurity also writ large upon the face of the weavers as majority of them are illiterate. Agriculture being the main occupation the weavers lacked confidence in their social set ups as compared with their female counterparts of the urban areas. Therefore by giving economic security through greater promotion of handloom sector she can gain socio-economic security in the midst of male dominated patriarchal system. The needs of women should be dealt from the grass root levels. By implications it means that the Tangkhuls are traditionally with rural background. (Zehol, Lucy, 1998). However with the passage of time like any other Tribal societies, the Tangkhul society is also passing through a time of transition – rom Tradition to Modernity. We see women working side by side with men in all kinds of jobs. (Mao, John, 1998). This itself implies the status of women as an encouraging trend emerging in the modern period. Very recently the spiritual leader Dalai Lama has voiced his opinion that that a woman understands the needs of others more sensitively and therein female should make a more important role and thus women should take more active role with self confidence as quoted in the state dailies' *The People's Chronicle,* 3 May, 2013.

Problems Faced

Some of the main problems faced by the women producers are given:

Having discussed some of the basic problems confronting in the region some major problems could be pointed out for further action plan so that a progressive weaving plan scheme could be choked out in the future.

(i) Traditional practices of weaving cloths are still practiced mostly in Ukhrul which makes decrease in productivity and increase in wastage of unnecessary time during weaving. Despite their potentiality women find it hard to rely on weaving as sustainable livelihood.

(ii) Quality colour, design and size are not well standardised as demand for both national and international market.

(iii) Lack of professional management among the weavers especially among the co-operate societies.

(iv) Inadequate quality and high price of imported raw materials.
(v) Outdated methods of weaving and low traditional efficiency.
(vi) Lack of financial support and credit facilities by the yarn decades.
(vii) Exploitation of weavers by the local yarn traders.

Some Suggested Measures

The following points have been suggested for effective implementation by the state Government and concern departments to solve the present prevailing problems.

1. Suitable organisation be set up to provide finance to the weaver outside the co operational fold to let them carry on their production activity and also to arrange an alternative mechanism for meeting the credit needs through formation of self help group (SHG) or other related society formed by the weavers themselves.
2. Already closed down Manipur spinning mill Ltd. Be make and revived to minimise the problems of shortages of handloom yarn to the weavers.
3. A central weavers union be established for conducting programmes in the use of improved appliances and training for weavers.
4. The state government should provide liberal financial assistance to the weavers in all the district to let them carry on with the profession without difficulty in the form of subsidies and loans with flat interest rates.
5. State machineries and agencies be appointed to arrange marketing of the cloth produced by them.
6. Most importantly the health care of the weavers should be given top priority as most of the weavers are marginalised farmers or otherwise small traders.
7. The life Insurance introduced by India under the Mahatma Gandhi Bunkar Bima Yojana for weavers health and education should be made to reach the target area. This should be aware publicly to all the weavers in all the right producers so that the weavers and their family are not suffered unnecessarily.

8. Lastly, more fairs and festivals at the district headquarter should be encourage and promoted by the state govt. and other funding agencies to exhibit and showcase handloom products by inviting all the weavers from different villages of the district. A cash award and certificate can be given to the best weavers to boost the morale and strength of the weavers. This will definitely encourage the weavers to further accelerate the growth of their potential.

End Note

With colourful ethnicity in diverse colours and hues in spite of so many difficulties, handloom is one of the main sources of household economy. Various designs and traditional patterns of handloom clothes can definitely propel even outside the state as the demands of handloom cloths are highly in demand. One unique characteristic features about Manipur/Ukhrul handloom are the production of 'phanek' which is not produced by mills. With various products of handloom cloth in the state, there is huge demand outside the state & even has a huge potentials for export.

Thus, the future prospects of the women in Manipur and the Tangkhul Women in particular, handloom industry has bright future prospects provided sustained efforts are made for making it progressive taking special advantage of accommodating Handloom Production in the Free Trade Agreement (FTA) between India and Myanmar, it leaves ample scope for strengthening the economic condition of the women and gives social security towards the attainment of social recognition in the national/International realm of future development. And in due process it will strengthen the economic ties of Manipur with the rest of the world through furtherance of the 'Look-East-Policy' of the Indian Government for future Development. The state Govt. should also give more emphasis on state tariffs. The recent handloom exhibition at Myanmar under the sponsorship of the state Handloom Corporation and Tourism Department headed by the state chief Minister should be an eye opener for the women weavers leaving in the hill areas of Manipur. They should learn to grab the opportunity of globalisation in the midst of growing Trade Policies by different sectors. The state political machineries need to focus on equal distribution assets and wealth and gender equity at the same time.

References

1. Amar Yumnam, and E. Bijoy (2011); "Economic Development of North Eastern Region of India". in Amar (Ed.) *Northeast India Selected Regional Issues*. Akansha Publishing House, New Delhi and MU Publication.

2. A. Rajmani Singh and Babhuti B. Pradhan (1998); "Sociological Constraints in the Economic Development of Manipur, from Wikipedia. the free Encyclopedia. *Society*. A Regency Publication, New Delhi.
3. Bhatia and Bhatia (2000); 'Theories and Principles of Education: (Philosophical and Sociological Bases of Education)'. Doaba House, Delhi.
4. Chongloi, Paotinlen (2011); "Business Opportunities with special reference to Northeast India and realising strategies towards the Look East Policy," *Journal of Northeast India studies,* Vol. 1, No. 1, July, 2011, pp. 88-89. (c) 2011 JNEIS
5. Eyingbeni Humtsoe, (2010); "Beyond the Kitchen and the Pew: Naga Women and Leadership Roles". in Zuchamo Yanthan, et al. (Ed) *Nagas Today: Indigenous Discourse*. Naga Students' Union, Delhi Publication, India.
6. Govt. of Manipur (2011); "Manipur Tourism Policy, 2011"; Department of Tourism.
7. Hudson, T.C. (1911); 'The Naga Tribes of Manipur'. Low Price Publication, New Delhi.
8. Horam, M. (1977); 'Social and Cultural Life of Nagas". Low Price Publication, New Delhi.
9. June, 2011. V.V. Giri National Labour Institute Retrieved: 22/11/2012.
10. Kshetrimayum, Otajit (2011); "Rethinking Co operative in Rural Development; A case study of Handloom Weavers Cooperatives in Manipur." *Labour & Development*, Vol.
11. Lucy Jajo and Binota (2012); "Prospects and Opportunities of Community Based Tourism in Northeast India: A Case Study of Ukhrul, Manipur" in Sarkar, *et al.*, (Ed.) *Sustainable Tourism: Issues and Challenges.* MacMillan Publishers India Ltd.
12. LucyJajo and Binota (2012); "Shirui-lily: A Hidden Tourist Destination Ukhrul in Northeast India. (Community Based Tourism Perspectives)". In Ashok Aima *et al.* (Ed), *Tourism Destination Management: Strategic Practices and Policies.* Kanishka Publishers. New Delhi.
13. Mao, John (1998); Status of Tribal Women in General" in Zehol (ed.) *Women in Naga Society*. A Regency Publication, New Delhi.
14. Singh and Sharma (2008); *Handlooms of Manipur: (Problems & Prospects)*, Unnat Publications, Lucknow.
15. Sundarapandian, M. (2002); " Growth & Prospects of Handloom Sector in India" in *National Bank for Agriculture and rural Development; NABARD,* Deptt. of Economic Analysis and Research, Bandura (East), Mumbai, p. 8121.
16. Singh, M. Bishwanath (2005); "Report on North-East India the Development Paradigm" *Journal of Northeast India Studies*.
17. Singh, M. Vishwanath, (2005); "Report on Northeast India: The Development Paradigm" in mbiswanath@yahoo.com.
18. Verma, Sawakia Bihari, *et al.*, (2008), "Better Quality of Rural Life",

Northeast Regions, Tribal, Delhi Areas. Vol II; Sarup & Sons Darya Ganj; New Delhi.

19. Chronicle Bureau (2013); 'State Handloom and Crafts Exhibitions in Mandalay' in the *People's Chronicles*. Vol. 1, 17th Feb.
20. Zehol, Lucy (1998); The Tangkhul Women Today" in Zehol (ed) *Women in Naga Society*. A Regency Publication, New Delhi.

11

Right to Education (RTE) Act 2009

Its Relevance in Manipur

Thothuingam Shinglai

> *"No community with an illiterate family, nor a family with an illiterate person."*

Attainment of universal primary education is one of the Millennium Development Goals of the United Nations targeted to be achieved by the year 2015, which is unlikely given the present 74.04 per cent literates in India (Census, 2011). If the goal of universalization of elementary education is to be achieved, there is a strong need for an enrolment drive and an action plan to ensure the attendance and retention of those enrolled. Introduction of RTE is seen as a positive move, a step closure in thousands of miles journey towards universal primary education and the worst, it did not guarantee quality education. There are now more schools, colleges, universities and other institutions than ever before and still counting, more persons attend such institutions at present than at any time in the past. The problems in education have never been so acute than present challenges, be it un-enrolment, dropout rates, closing the gap of gender disparities in education and junk of quality issues need to be addressed. Policies and plans for development are evolving at the best possible level. In order to meet the need of society, education produces work force with the type of personality, attitudes and values required best for thriving, which is manufactured in the form of hidden curriculum (no say on syllabus, it is decided by.... for the students).

The expansion of education began in those countries that first experienced industrial revolution, Britain, France and United States, where it was also accompanied with changes in the socio-economic and political orders. In the modern world, there is hardly any country that would not like to have a comprehensive and inclusive system of education, India is not an exception. Yet the expansion of education has not followed the same course everywhere, and for a big country like India, it has been highly uneven. Accessing education is not easy under all circumstances, not only on account of severe economic inequalities, but also because of strong and deeply-rooted social prejudices against women and disadvantages communities.

Historical Survey on Education

With the Regulating Act of 1773, the Government of India is said to have been born, with the designated Governor in Council of Bengal. The Governor-General of Bengal did little to control or direct the educational policies of the other parts of India. At this time, therefore, 'education' may be said to have been a 'provincial' matter, subject only to the distant coordinating authority of the Court of Directors in England.

The Charter Act of 1833 introduced a unitary system of Government. All the revenues were raised in the name of the Central Government and all expenditure needed its approval. The Provincial Governments could not spend even one rupee or create a post, however small, without the approval of the Government of India, which also was the only law-making body for the country as a whole. In other words, all executive, financial and legislative authorities were exclusively vested in the Central Government and the Provinces merely acted as its agents. Education, thus, became a provincial subject for purpose of day to day administration. But it has to be remembered that the Central Government retained large power of control.

One of the major educational controversies today refers to the role of the Government of India in education. With the adoption of Five Year Plans and the creation of the Planning Commission, the real authority to determine policies, priorities and programmes has now passed on from the States to the Centre in most sectors of development. Under the initial Sarva Shiksha Abhiyan (SSA) framework (2004), the fund sharing pattern of GoI: States during the X plan was 75:25. It was revised during the XI plan, increasing the State's share gradually in a phased manner. Thus, for FY 2007-09 (65:35), FY 2009-10 (60:40), FY 2010-11 (55:45) and FY 2011-12 (50:50). For the North-East, the Centre and States share remains 90:10 during the entire XI Plan period. (SSA, 2009:40) This has been agreed at 35:65 between States and Centre, though state governments continue to argue that their share should be lower. It is alleged that the educational progress in the States is now more dependent upon the financial allocations and priorities decided at the Centre by the Planning Commission and the Ministry of Education than upon any decision taken by the States at their own level. In short, the States understanding about their needs in education has been overshadowed by the process of centralisation in policy making.

States claim that they understand their educational needs much better than the Centre; and the attempt of the Centre to cut into their sphere has generally done more harm than good to the health of education. They also assert that Central grants should be placed at the disposal of the States without any strings attached and the manner in which their proposals are scrutinised, modified or amended by the Centre while grants are being sanctioned is undesirable. On the other end, the Centre complains that its genuine selfless desire to help the States is misunderstood as interference, 'indirect pressures' or as 'leading strings', that the States do not appreciate the larger interests of education underlying the policies and programmes proposed by it; that the States do not often implement the sanctioned schemes in the manner in which they ought to be implemented; and that it often finds itself helpless to enforce the directives given by it. Education, as one understood in India, developed practically into a 'joint responsibility' of the Central and State Governments. But unfortunately, neither the States nor Centre is satisfied with the present position; each one of them has a number of charges to make against the other. From this, we can draw a conclusion that education has national importance and it demands contribution from every party cutting across boundaries.

The old distinctions between lower primary and upper primary, lower secondary and upper secondary disappeared in 1906 and the institutions were reclassified into elementary and secondary schools (Educational, 1906 Paras 2, 145). The purpose of the public elementary schools of India was "to form and strengthen the character and develop the intelligence of the children entrusted to it, and to make the best use of the school years available in assisting both girls and boys, according to their different needs to fit themselves practically as well as intellectually for the work of life (Samal, 1984:25).

Current Status of Education

There is a wide regional, gender and caste disparity in education, which is reflected in the literacy rates. The following tables will illustrate the current status of India's education. Looking at the data, one can have a fair understanding of what is happening at the education front.

Table 11.1: No. of illiterates in 2001 and 2011 Censuses of India

(in millions)

Year	*Persons*	*Males*	*Females*
2001	467.9	205.7	273.6
2011	431.8	179.6	252.2

Source: Census 2001, 2011.

The absolute number of 36.1 million illiterates declined between 2001 and 2011 Census out of which 16 million are males and 20.1 million females. The decline in illiterate females is higher than that of males; it could be due to various policies initiated focusing on improvement of female literacy. An important finding of 2011 Census count is that increase in female literacy is substantially higher than increase in male literacy in most of the districts, narrowing the gap of male and female literacy. Bihar has witnessed significant increase in female literacy followed by Uttar Pradesh due to several state specific basic education programmes.

Though improving literacy rate is a welcome note, there are still eleven states below national average, which need special treatment to minimize the gap. Target group approach and special treatment to those lower rung without omitting the other states to retain their

Table 11.2: India's Literacy Rate (%) 1951-2011

Census years	*Total*	*Male*	*Female*
1951	18.33	27.16	8.86
1961	28.30	40.40	15.35
1971	34.45	45.96	21.97
1981	43.57	56.38	29.76
1991	52.21	64.13	39.29
2001	64.84	75.26	53.67
2011	74.04	82.14	65.46

Source: Census of India since Independence.

growth remain a challenge to the inclusive growth propagating nation. The comparison between the two extremes, highest literate state Kerala 93.91 and lowest literate state Bihar 63.83 gave us the disparity, which is far from satisfactory, irrespective of what they teach and how they teach.

Table 11.3: Increase in Literacy in Per cent Points from Census 1991-2011

Censuses	*Total Literacy*	*Male Literacy*	*Female Literacy*	*Male Female gap in Literacy*
1991-2001	13.3	11.7	14.9	24.8
2001-2011	9.0	6.34	11.26	16.68

Source: Census 1991, 2001 and 2011.

The Planning Commission target of reducing the gender gap in education to 10 per cent points by 2011-2012 falls short by 6.68 per cent points.

Critical Analysis of the Main Features of RTE

> *"No Child Working, Every Child in School and Learning Well" Pratham Vision."*

At the World Conference on Education for All (EFA), as many as 155 member states of the UN assembled at Jomtien, Thailand in 1990 and firmly pledged to provide education for all by 2000, which has utterly failed.

The right to education is a law in Article 26 of the Universal Declaration of Human Rights and Articles 13 and 14 of the International Covenant on Economic, Social and Cultural Rights.

According to the International Covenant on Economic, Social and Cultural Rights, the right to education includes the right to free compulsory primary education for all. The right to education also includes a responsibility to provide basic education for individuals, who have not completed primary education. In addition to these, there are also access to education provisions, and an obligation to eliminate discrimination at all levels of the educational system.

The right to education is recognised in many national constitutions and is considered as national importance, including the Belgian Constitution (former article 17, now article 24), Indian Constitution (Under article 21(a)) and the Dutch Constitution (article 23).

The Directive Principle (Article 45) originally enshrined in the Constitution of India in 1950 stated that "the State shall endeavour to provide within a period of 10 years from the commencement of this Constitution, for free and compulsory education for all children until they complete the age of 14 years", but it could not effectively 'direct' the state to universalise elementary education.

As that deadline was about to be passed many decades ago, the education minister at that time, M.C. Chagla, said, "Our Constitution fathers did not intend that we just set up hovels, put students there, give untrained teachers, give them bad textbooks, no playgrounds, and say, we have complied with Article 45 and primary education is expanding... they meant that real education should be given to our children between the ages of 6 and 14" (Chagla, 1964). The RTE bill was approved by the cabinet on 2 July 2009. Rajya Sabha passed the bill on 20 July 2009 and the Lok Sabha on 4 August 2009. It received Presidential assent and was notified as law on 3 Sept. 2009 as *The Childrens' Right to Free and Compulsory Education Act*. The law came into effect in the whole of India except the state of Jammu and Kashmir from 1 April 2010, if the State does not comply with all the provision of the Act, within the stipulated timeframe, any citizen can take the State to court. The justiciability of the RTE Act will be tested after March 2013. It will be interesting to know where and on what grounds the first such cases will be filed and how the State responds to the cases.

For the first time in the history of India, a law was brought into force by a Prime Minister speech. It stated, "We are committed to ensuring that all children, irrespective of gender and social category, have access to education. An education that enables them to acquire the skills, knowledge, values and attitudes necessary to become responsible and active citizens of India."

The Act has seven chapters and eight parts and deals with the duties of centre, appropriate government, local authority and parents. It also provided details on the responsibility of schools and teachers, curriculum and completion of elementary education and protection of rights of child. Well-known educationist Anil Sadagopa said that RTE is a hurriedly-drafted Act.

Free and compulsory education was made a fundamental right under Article 21 of the Constitution in December 2002, by the 86th Amendment. In translating this into action, the 'Right of Children to Free and Compulsory Education Bill' was drafted in 2005. This was revised and became an Act in August 2009, but was not notified for about seven months. Until now, elementary education (Class I to VIII) in India is neither free nor compulsory. 'Free' education is defined to refer to only tuition fee-free education. The bill goes a little bit forward, and states that free education should mean that no fees or charges of any kind are levied on students. The bill also states that free education may include provision of textbooks, stationery, uniforms, public transport, (schools shall be establish within one km of walking distance for class I-V and three km for class V to VII; but the inclusion of public transport indicates the apprehension of planner from falling short of the provision) school meal, etc., to the school children so that "freedom for the parent or guardian from liability to incur expenditure" is ensured, but "subject to rules made in this behalf." This only offers an opportunity for the government to disregard these provisions.

"Compulsory elementary education" is an obligation and the essence of the Right to Education Act is reflected in it. Under the name of education, presently all forms of education are being allowed. The bill has to define that education means formal schooling, and not non-formal education.

As per the age criteria, 6 to 14 years old are eligible for free education, but the Act itself stated that free education shall be entitled till completion of elementary education even after completion of 14 years of age. Upper age limit is added to incorporate Child Labour Act; 14 years of age in RTE has no bearing effect on elementary education.

Despite high enrolment rates of approximately 95 per cent as per the Annual Status of Education Report (ASER 2009), 52.8 per cent of children studying in fifth grade lack the reading skills expected at second grade.

The term, child in the RTE Act referred to males and females of 6 to 14 years of age, but the recent Census of India (2011) goes beyond this gender and included "Male, Female and Others", (first time in the world history). The RTE Act needs to be more inclusive.

Role of State/local Government: Article 8 (a) states that the role of state government is to ensure free and compulsory education for all children until the completion of elementary education. Northeast states present a specific picture that appears to call for region specific strategies to strengthen the enabling conditions for quality (SSA, 2009:29). Infrastructures in many parts of the NE remain unsatisfactory and physical access to schools continues to be vulnerable especially during rainy weather.

According to Sarva Shiksha Abhiyan July 2009 report, Manipur stands out for doing no progress or any kind of trainings (three training under SSA, 20 days in service training each year, 30 days induction training and 60 days training for untrained teachers) and no reporting on the distribution of textbooks, teacher grants or school grants (SSA, 2009:30).

Opening new primary and upper primary schools as per the norms and standard laid down by RTE Act includes availability of library, learning and teaching equipments and all weather school building, availability of drinking water and toilets. These facilities are not seen in many of the present schools; there is humongous task due in this aspect too. The need of the hour is to implement RTE at the established schools and upgrade them, rather than focusing on new buildings. This will minimise the cost and space usage.

School Management Committees (SMCs)

By the Act, SMCs are to comprise of mostly parents (three fourth of the committee) and are to be responsible for planning and managing the operations of government and aided schools. SMCs will help increase the accountability of government schools, but SMCs for government schools need to be given greater powers over evaluation of teacher competencies and students learning assessment. Women's ratio in the committee should be fifty per cent is a welcome note.

Teachers: In the RTE Act, proper disciplinary channels for teachers have not been defined. The School Management Committees need to be given this power to allow speedy disciplinary action at the local level. Performance based pay scales need to be considered as a way to improve teaching.

The Act is excessively input-focused rather than outcomes-oriented. Even though better school facilities, books, uniforms and better qualified teachers are important, their significance in the Act has been overestimated in the light of inefficient, corrupt and unaccountable institutions of education provision.

The stringent provisions of the Act make it mandatory for all children to produce income and caste certificates, BPL cards and birth certificates. Orphan children are often unable to produce such documents, even though they are willing to do so. As a result, schools may not admit them, as they require the documents as a condition to admission.

Among all the components, the RTE Act seems to be least sensitive to growing inequalities in the education system. It does not discourage the growth of the fee-charging private school system. 25 per cent reservation in private schools can be understood as an attempt of the government to interfere in the functioning of private institutions in order to control them. The RTE Act, 2009 clause 12(1)(c) mandates the private schools to reserve at least 25 per cent of their seats for economically weaker and socially disadvantaged sections in the entry level class. The constitutional validity of this clause was challenged in the apex court of the country. However on 12, April 2012, a bench of Chief Justice S.H. Kapadia, Justice K.S. Radhakrishnan and Swatanter Kumar upheld the constitutional validity of the Act. Private schools will receive reimbursements from the government calculated on the basis of per-child expenditure in government schools. How will 'weaker and disadvantaged sections' be defined and verified is not clear. For Manipur state, income below Rs. 40,000 is set as defining economically backward apart from SC/ST category, but the fact that income certificates are not regulated and verified strictly, the chances of manipulation is very high. How will the government monitor the whole process, needs to be addressed. Some private schools are very reputed and provide good quality of education and some are either at par with government schools or little ahead. There is a hierarchy of private schools, which are stratified in terms of quality education. Who will go where, what will be the criteria for that is unanswered.

What will the State do with all the private, unaided schools, that do not measure up to the standards set out in the RTE Act for buildings and playgrounds by March 2013? How will the State respond to those government schools that are not able to measure up to the standards of the RTE Act by March 2013? With the shrinking urban space, how and where will the government build schools and playgrounds as stated in the RTE Act remained doubtful.

The amount put aside by then Finance Minister, Pranab Mukherjee, for the Sarva Shiksha Abhiyan is only Rs. 25,555 crores for 2012-13, which falls short of the recommended financial requirement of Rs. 1.82 lakh crore. From where will the rest of amount come? The centre's inability to meet its own proposed allocations on education as well as protests from states reveal the lackadaisical attitude that persists towards elementary education.

There has been substantial progress in increasing enrolment with national average now at 98.3 per cent (2009-2010) according to official statistics. However, the attendance of pupils in class rooms has declined. In 2007, 73.4 per cent students enrolled for Standards I-IV/V were present in class, which has fallen to 70.9 per cent by 2011 (EPW, 2012). Long absence and irregular attendance are early warning for potential dropout and more focus on attendance data is needed.

Further, the Act has provision to have a pupil-teacher ratio, one teacher per 30 students in primary and one teacher per 35 students in upper primary classes. The Act felt the need to provide one head teacher only when there are more than 150 students in primary and 100 students in upper primary, this has the potential to convey wrong message and schools having head teacher may continue to attract more number of students. Every school requires head teacher to ensure proper attendance of the teachers. While several committees and experts have recently recommended for reduction of number of students per teacher on an average of 1:25 these suggestions have not been incorporated.

Implementation Mechanism

The National Commission for Protection of Child Rights (NCPCR) has been designated as the agency to monitor provisions of the Right to Free and Compulsory Education (RTE) Act. To ensure that the RTE Act is implemented successfully in letter and spirit, consensus among institutions, government departments, civil society and other stakeholders has been initiated. It has instituted an expert committee comprising officials from various government departments and would be coordinated by two Commissioners and assisted by a separate staff in all its activities. This division would establish links with the Ministry of Human Resource Development (MHRD).

It has suggested the appointment of state representatives to act as the "eyes and ears" of the NCPCR in different states. These representatives would be members of civil society with experience in the field of education, the criteria "experience in the field of education" varies and the lacuna of not having specific qualification may result in lack of quality information dissemination and reporting. They will also facilitate follow up of complaints received from their state, which is a serious concern.

The RTE Act has special implications for the Child Labour Act and the Ministry of Labour has a role to play. Similarly, schools run by the Tribal Affairs Ministry will also come under the purview of the RTE. Ministries that are affected by the RTE Act, such as the Ministry of Social Justice and Empowerment, Labour Ministry, Tribal Affairs Ministry and Ministry of Panchayati Raj need to coordinate in order to benefit children from RTE. It is important that there is smooth coordination and communication between NCPCR and these ministries. NCPCR has to coordinate with other national commissions like the National Commission for Women, National Commission for Scheduled Castes and Scheduled Tribes on how to work together and ensure that girls or children from marginalized communities are not denied the right to education. However, for better implementation and monitoring of the Act, there needs to be greater awareness in the country, so that its provisions are understood and incorporated by all institutions. In order to do so, a massive publicity campaign will have to be undertaken, including translation of the Act into different languages, perhaps jointly with MHRD and other agencies.

Present status of implementation: Since RTE Act came into force on 1st April 2010, 50,672 new schools, 4.98 lakh additional classrooms, 6.31 lakh teachers, etc. have been sanctioned to States and UTs under Sarva Shiksha Abhiyan (SSA) (merely sanction did not ensure their implementation). As on December 5, 2011, only 27 States have notified the State Rules under the RTE Act, including five Union Territories, which have adopted the Central RTE Rules. Arunachal Pradesh, Assam, Manipur, Meghalaya, Mizoram, Nagaland and Sikkim states are among them.

The States of Karnataka, Gujarat, West Bengal, Goa, Delhi, Puducherry, Uttarakhand have not yet notified the RTE rules, and these States have been asked to expedite the notification of the State RTE rules (B. Zutsi and Ramakant, 2012:34). How long will it take for complete implementation of the Act has not been discussed in the Act.

Table 11.5: The RTE Act mandates the following activity and timeframe

Activity	*Timeframe*
Establishment of neighbourhood schools	3 years (by 31st March, 2013)
Provision of school infrastructure	3 years (by 31st March, 2013)
All weather school buildings, One-classroom-one-teacher. Head Teacher-cum-Office room. Library, Toilets, drinking water, Barrier free access, Playground, fencing, boundary walls	
Provision of teachers as per prescribed Pupil Teacher Ratio	3 years (by 31st March, 2013)
Training of untrained teachers	5 years (by 31st March 2015)
Quality interventions and other provisions	With immediate effect

There are a whole host of issues that will crop up for the Government to address by March 31st, 2013.

Measures and Suggestions

Despite the flaws in the RTE Act, it is equally important for us to simultaneously ensure its proper implementation.

1. RTE Act should be translated into regional dialects for wider awareness and to ensure proper understanding, including a simplified version of the Act, posters, primers and pamphlets describing the basic provisions and rights. Designing special material for children, so that they also understand the Act.
2. Centre should monitor states' role and ensure that: (a) availability; (b) accessibility; (c) acceptability; and (d) adaptability, irrespective of regional disadvantages is fulfilled.
3. Instead of building new schools and spending huge amount, revamp and encourage the private schools through monetary assistance to rise up to RTE provision standard.
4. Schools need to be made aware of provisions of the 25 per cent reservations, and the role of School Managing Committee. This can be undertaken through mass awareness programmes as well as ensuring proper understanding by stakeholders responsible for its implementation.
5. It is likely that once the Act is notified, a number of different groups affected by this Act will challenge it in the court. It is, therefore, critically important for us to follow such cases and bring to the public domain without jeopardizing the implementation of the Act.
6. Ministry of Human Resource Development latest report on dropout rate of school children is 2.8 million. Slightly less than 50 per cent of the total were never enrolled and slightly more than 50 per cent are dropout. In order to ensure retention of the enrolled students and to attract new students, the school should incorporate outside class room learning activities, such as free and compulsory environment exposure trips.
7. Since we are dealing with children, it is necessary to incorporate what they like, such as painting, music, dance and games.
8. Face to face interview of teachers by competent authority, preferably inter-state interview whereby one state board will interview the other state teacher to avoid family and friends favour in appointment, especially of those whose educational qualification are not satisfactory.
9. The RTE has provision for children with special needs. So,

with more enrolment, the number of children, who need special care is likely to increase, and there should be readied mechanisms to tackle, in the form of arranging extra teacher to attend.

Conclusion

Progress in increasing access to elementary education in India since independence has been improving, but steady. However, access to education and achievement in education are different. Over the coming years, greater emphasis is likely to be on learning outcomes and improvements in the quality of learning experience in elementary education. Inequalities between those, who have accessed and those, who have not accessed will remain, and disparity in educational achievement is likely to be intensified. The achievement of education for all at the elementary level and the reduction of inequalities in access to secondary and higher education will require considerable political will at all levels of the Indian polity.

To establish a knowledge society, "without fear or favour", education has to be prioritised along with increases in public spending. There are many other loopholes, which are pressing and challenging in the way of RTE: quality education, funding, teacher skills and enhancement of reservation policy are some major concerns. A critical development in 2011 has been the decision taken in principle to extend the right to education till Class X (age 16). This is likely to compound the existing difficulties if implemented.

References

Adiseshiah, M. (1997). Foreword to Naik, J.P. (1997). *The Education Commission and After*. New Delhi, 2nd Edition A.P.H. Publishing Corporation.

Aggarwal, Y. (2000). 'Which districts benefited the most from DPEP?', *DPEP Newsletter,* Nov 2000, pp. 5-9.

Alexander, R.J. (2001). *Culture and Pedagogy: International Comparisons in Primary Education*, Oxford: Blackwell.

Basu, A. (1978). Policy and Conflict in India: The Reality and Perception of Education, in Altbach, P.G. and Kelly, G.P. *Education and Colonialism*, New York and London: Longman.

Bhupinder, Zutsi and Ramakant, R. (2012). *Status of Elementary Education in India.* Pantagon Press, New Delhi.

Bandyopadhyay, M. and Subrahmanian, R. (2008). *Gender Equity in Education: A Review of Trends and Factors*, CREATE Research Monograph 18. Delhi/ Sussex.

Blum, N. and Diwan, R. (2007). *Small, Multigrade Schools and Increasing Access to Primary Education in India: National Context and NGO Initiatives,* CREATE Research Monograph 17, London/Delhi/Sussex.

Chavan, M. (2009). 'Is it working?' *Annual Status of Education Report (Rural) 2008*, New Delhi, Pratham Resource Centre.

Colclough, C. and De A. (2010). 'The Impact of Aid on Education Policy in India', *International Journal of Educational Development* 30, 5, pp. 497-507.

Dighe, A. (2002). 'Social Mobilization and Total Literacy Campaigns' in Govinda, R. (ed.) *India Education Report: A Profile of Basic Education.* New Delhi: NIEPA.

Dyer, C. (2000). *Operation Blackboard: Policy Implementation in Indian Elementary Education.* Oxford: Symposium Books.

Drèze, J. and Kingdon, G.G. (2001). School Participation in Rural India, *Review of Development Economics*, 5, 1, 1-24.

Drèze, J. and Sen, A. (2005). *India: Economic Development and Participation*, New Delhi, Oxford University Press.

GoI (1998). National Policy on Education 1086 (as modified in 1992) with National Policy on Education 1968, New Delhi: Department of Education, Ministry of Human Resource Development.

Government of Manipur: *Educational Department Notification*, 21st October 2010. Retrieved 2012-09-11.

Grindle, M. (2004). *Despite the Odds: The Contentious Politics of Education Reform*. Princeton: Princeton University Press.

Kingdon, G. and Muzammil, M. (2003). *The Political Economy of Education in India*, Delhi: Oxford University Press.

Kumar, K. (2005). *Political Agenda of Education: A Study of Colonialist and Nationalist Ideas*. 2nd edition, New Delhi: Sage Publication.

Kumar, K. and Sarangapani, P.M. (2004). 'History of Quality Debate', *Contemporary Education Dialogue,* 2(1), Monsoon issue, pp. 30-52.

Kumar, K. (2010). 'Quality in Education: Competing Concepts' *Contemporary Education Dialogue,* 7(1) pp. 7-18.

Mathur, K. (2001). 'Does Performance Matter? Policy Struggles in Education', *Journal of Educational Planning and Administration*, XV (2), pp. 225-240.

Naik, J.P. (1966). *Elementary Education in India: The Unfinished Business,* London: Asia Publishing House.

Naik, J.P. (1997). *The Education Commission and After*. New Delhi, 2nd Edition A.P.H. Publishing Corporation.

National Council of Educational Research and Training (1965). *Second All-*

India Educational Survey. New Delhi: National Council of Educational Research and Training.

Pratham (2009). *Annual Status of Education Report (Rural) 2008*, New Delhi: Pratham Resource Centre.

PROBE (1999). Public Report on Basic Education in India. New Delhi: Oxford University Press.

"Right to Education Bill 2009" (PDF). Retrieved 2012-09-11.

SSA (2010a). Sarva Shiksa Abhiyan, A Programme for Universal Elementary Education Framework for Implementation, http://www.education.nic.in/ssa/ssa_1.asp Accessed July 24th 2012.

SSA (2010b). National Programme for Education of Girls at Elementary Level (NPEGEL) http://ssa.nic.in/girls-education/npegel. July 24th 2012.

Subrahmanian, R. (2005). 'Educational Exclusion and the Developmental State', in Chopra.

R. and Jeffery, P. *Educational Regimes in Contemporary India*, New Delhi: Sage Publications India.

Supreme Court upholds constitutional validity of RTE Act". *The Hindu*. 12 April 2012. Retrieved 3 Sept. 2012.

Velaskar P. (2010). 'Quality and Inequality in Indian Education: Some critical policy concerns' *Contemporary Education Dialogue*, 7(1), pp. 58-93.

12

Education and Identity Formation

Some Reflections on the History of the Nagas of Chandel District (With Special Reference to the Monsang Nagas)

W. Somie Monsang

Situated at the gateway to Myanmar and Southeast Asian countries, Chandel district holds an important geo-political position in India's look east policy. Chandel district is also a strategic hub for many underground groups, although the majority is shared by the NSCN (I-M), i.e., the National Socialist Council of Nagalim (Isak-Muivah). In present time, the district is inhabited by many ethnic groups, largely Nagas, namely, Anal, Chothe, Lamkang, Monsang, Moyon, Maring, and Tarao. The other 'tribes' inhabiting Chandel are Aimol, Kom, Thadou, Vaiphai, and Zou.

The Anal, Lamkang, Monsang and Moyon Nagas are generally referred to as 'allied tribes' because of their close historical and cultural affinities. Despite their close cultural affinities, each of them, however, has evolved a distinctive identity long before the arrival of the British colonial powers in the country. Though the early existence of some 'tribes', like Monsang was virtually ignored in the colonial accounts of the 'tribes' inhabiting Manipur, the ethnic identity of 'tribes', like Anal and Lamkang, was projected with misrepresentations devoid of historical evidence. It is pertinent, therefore, to question as to why the colonial ethnographers or writers were silent on the existence of the Monsang community on the one hand, and, on the other, why were its sibling tribes, like Anal, Lamkang and Moyon, misrepresented. In his

Gazetteer of Manipur (1886), Captain E.W. Dun treated the Monsangs as Anal, he identified 'Mansang' as "an Anal village in South-Eastern Manipur," thereby clubbing the Monsang Naga tribe with the dominant Anal Naga tribe (Dun, 1886:159). Other than E.W. Dun, apparently none of the colonial writers or ethnographers took note of the tribe (Monsang). G.A. Grierson's *Linguistic Survey of India* (1904), totally missed out the Monsang tribe and their language affinities, even as he talked about the languages of the neighbouring tribes – Anal and Lamkang. The small population of the Monsang Nagas could be one possible reason. As the population of the Monsang Nagas was comparatively smaller, and that is why they were subsumed or clubbed together with the adjoining dominant tribes, which showed close resemblance to them. This was perhaps the reason why Dun erroneously considered Mansang or Monsang as an Anal village. Such observations need to be reviewed in the light of the existence of the Monsang as a distinct community having its own language despite sharing close resemblance and affinities with the Anal Nagas.

It is presumed that the failure on the part of the colonial officials to acknowledge the cultural distinctiveness of each community and their ethnic identity was due to their limited knowledge about the concerned 'tribes'. Such limitation of knowledge and understanding of the communities are bound to arise as most of the information pertaining to these people seems to have been derived without proper in-depth study. In fact, the present Chandel district, lying towards the south eastern part of Manipur and inhabited by allied tribes, was least considered and attended to by the colonial officials as compared to other regions in present day Manipur. Whether this was due to inaccessibility or lack of interest is uncertain. Whatever might have been the reason, it is clear that the colonial officials failed to identify and differentiate the already existing groups under different nomenclatures speaking different languages and having their respective unique cultural heritages even as they shared close affinities with one another.

Ethnicity/Identity

Ethnicity and identity are often debated issues in many parts of the world. The ethnicity of the Naga tribes in present Chandel district suffers from similar conundrum. The failure to incorporate the native's socio-cultural history seemingly appears to complicate the whole problem. This is because, people's ideas regarding their identity or ethnicity differ from what has been perceived and written about them by outsiders.

Although mention of the Monsang Nagas is virtually absent in colonial accounts, other neighbouring tribes, like the Anal and Lamkang, are occasionally mentioned. However, the Anal tribe is sometimes mentioned as Naga, and at other times, they are referred to as an old Kuki sub-group. Interestingly, the allied tribes are also sometimes referred to as 'intermediary groups' falling somewhere between the Kuki and the Naga family. In the past few years, some writers even began to use terms like 'bridge-buffer' communities and 'trans-border' tribes to signify the Chandel Naga 'tribes' because of the geographical locations of their villages/countries. All these categories cannot be, but the creation of outsiders in their attempt to portray the communities according to their own studies, understanding and perception.

In the nineteenth century, an English surveyor, Captain R.P. Pemberton, mentioned the "Anal and Moyon as Naga tribes occupying the southern region by which the southern extremity of the Kuboo valley might be entered" (Pemberton, 1835:56). A contemporary of Pemberton, Lt. Col. McCulloch, one of the early British Political Agents in Manipur, talks about the "south-east part of the country, which received the name Anal Namphou from the two largest villages among them" (McCulloch, 1859:51). Later, in 1886, Captain E.W. Dun (in his *Gazetteer of Manipur*) mentioned Anal as a division of old Kuki tribe, a shift from the earlier views. Despite clubbing the Anal as part of the old Kuki tribe, Dun distinguishes "Anal Namfaw or *Anal people* as more civilized and intelligent than the Kongjai Kukis" (Dun, 1886: 70). In his *Statistical Accounts of Manipur* (1893), R. Brown, another British Political Agent in Manipur, observed that "these people (Anal) say that they came from a position south of the present one, and they celebrate in their songs the beauty of the land of their origin" (Brown, 1893:50).

By the turn of the twentieth century, tribes, like Anal and Lamkang, came to be recorded in other works. For instance, in *Linguistic Survey of India*, Grierson mentions the Anal and Lamkang as old-Kuki group. But later, he changed his view and asserted that Anal and Lamkang show a closer connection with the Naga languages than the dialects of the Kuki-Chin group (Grierson, 1904:9). This suggests that the colonial understanding of the ethnicity of the tribes, like Anal and Lamkang, was neither consistent nor clear. The other work that mentions Anal and Lamkang as part of the old Kuki clans is that of Lt. Colonel J. Shakespear. In his work entitled *The Lushai Kuki Clans*, Shakespear included Aimol, Anal, Chothe, Chiru, Kom, Lamkang, and Purum as belonging to old Kuki clans (Shakespear, 1912:47). This perception seems to lack historical basis, particularly in the case of the Anal and Lamkang tribes.

It is interesting to note that the use of the term 'old Kuki', believed to have originated somewhere by the end of the eighteenth century in Cachar (Steward, 1885:185), is relatively young as compared to the tribes like Anal, Monsang, and Moyon, which are mentioned in the *Cheitharol Kumbaba* (Royal Chronicles of Manipur). The *Cheitharol Kumbaba*, which started recording history dating back to C. 33 C.E., describes the Anal or Anan as Nagas in the mid-sixteenth century (Singh 1967:5). The *Cheitharol Kumbaba* also mentions Monsang and Moyon. As per the chronicle, the Monsang-Moyon people had settlements inside Manipur and were in constant war with the Meiteis as early as 1580 A.D. (Iboongohal, 1967:20). Thus, considering their long existence in Manipur, the application of the term 'old Kuki', which is a late eighteenth century phenomenon, to the allied tribes, like Anal, Monsang, Moyon and Lamkang, is historically anachronistic.

From the colonial perspective, the similarity in language was an important major yardstick in determining the ethnicity of groups. While some authors, like John Shakespear, attempted to study different aspects of cultural similarity and practices among the different groups, which became difficult and yielded little results. This draws our attention to understanding the factors as to why the allied tribes shared some similarities in language with the Chin-Lushais. Here, it is worth mentioning that for communities like the Anal, Monsang, Moyon and Lamkang, Naga historians (like Prof. Gangmumei) use terms, like '*Trans-border*' (Kabui, 1985:1), to signify the geographical area inhabited by them. The fact that the land inhabited by the tribes lies close to the Chin Hills of Burma in the south and the Kabow valley on the east explains why they have linguistic similarities with the Chin-Lushais. Such similar view is also shared by some Naga authors, like Shimmi Roland. According to Shimmi Roland, the similarity in language could be due to assimilation of language during the course of migration as the folksong of the above tribes suggest crossing Chin-Lushai hills at one point of time (Roland, 1988:63-64).

T.C. Hodson, the political agent in Manipur in his account of the Naga tribes of Manipur while speaking on various dialects of the region (Manipur), clearly mentioned that "it is clear that we have in this area (i.e. Manipur), a rich variety of dialects due to effect of the confluence of two, if not of three, streams of language" (Hodson, 1911:19). Seen in the light of this, the dialects spoken by Anal or for that matter Lamkang, Monsang and Moyon may have had their share of influence as well as impact from the Chin-Lushais. In fact, the history of the 'allied tribes' suggests that they had settled and crossed the Chin-Lushai hills at one point of time before coming to the present sites many centuries ago, during which assimilation and acculturation between different groups may probably have taken place. Rajendra Singh in his work (*Anals of Manipur*), mentions that the "Anal dialect is, no doubt, influenced by the Chin-Lushai languages during their long migratory stage and after reaching the present Manipur, it has been influenced by the Manipuri language" (Singh, 1981:49). It is in this context that we need to understand the dynamics of acculturation and assimilation of languages and cultures, which, however, does not necessarily mean that the interacting communities belong to the same ethnic group. In present day, Monsang language or for that matter Anal, Moyon and Lamkang languages have Manipuri influences; but it would be completely erroneous to suppose that they are of the same group/ethnicity.

Assertion of Identity from Native Perspectives

In the post-colonial period, and particularly in the last few decades, some of the early notions and perceptions regarding ethnicity of the allied tribes have been rectified by taking into account the views and opinions of the native peoples. For instance, K.S. Singh (in his *People of India*, 1998) states that the Anals identify themselves as one of the Naga groups and were also termed as Nagas during the census of

1951. M. Horam (in his work, *Naga Polity*, 1975) mentions as many as thirty-two known Naga tribes, which include the 'allied tribes'. Roland's *Comparative History of the Nagas from Ancient Period till 1826* (1998) clearly mentions that "the Anal were among the people, who migrated somewhere from China and said to have crossed the present Kachin and Kayan territories of Burma. Legends of the natives also tell that the ancestors of the Anal, and other Naga tribes as well, were among the primitive Nagas, who came out of the cave or earth hole situated in the north-east beyond the Naga Hills. As time went on, the Anal came into conflict with the Lushai-Kuki clans, who drove them South-east" (Roland, 1988:49).

Rajendra Singh (in his work, the *Anals of Manipur*) uses the term 'Pakan' to denote the 'allied tribes' on the basis of origin myths, cultural traits and language affinities. Whether the term 'Pakan' literally signifies the early ancestors or does it mean 'hill people' is not clear. Except for Anal, other communities have not been really expressive regarding the Pakan nomenclature. However, SR. Tohring, in her studies on the 'Identity of the Pakans', mentions that there are a number of folksongs and legends using the term 'Pakan' to denote the 'allied tribes'. They were separated into different groups and sub-groups before coming into contact with the Meeteis and other tribes (Tohring, 2001:14-15) There are legends current among the Nagas as regards their origin and migration; these traditions tell more about the migration within Manipur and the trans-Chindwin region" (Kabui, 1988:19).

During my field interviews with Monsang elders, many are of the strong view that they are Nagas. A similar feeling was also shared by many of the elders from neighbouring allied tribes. According to Monsang elders, except for certain linguistic affinities, most of the customary practices of the tribe are different from those of the Kukis. The village elders also point out that unlike the Kuki hereditary and autocratic village chief/king, among the Monsang Nagas, power and authority are shared by representation of different sub-clans in the village council, and forests and land in Monsang villages are shared by the entire village community as communal properties. Further, in the case of the Kukis, the house of the chief in the village was constructed much bigger and larger as compared to his fellow villagers, so as to indicate the position and status of the village chief. However, this custom was/is not practised in Monsang and her sister tribes.

The non-participation of the Chandel Nagas in the Kuki uprisings in Manipur in the early twentieth century is also suggestive of the fact that they did not consider themselves as Kukis even by then. During 1917-19, some of the tribes in Manipur volunteered as per the order issued and also imposed by the British government for the labour corps for France, which was being recruited from the hill tribes. The chiefs of the Kuki tribes resented this and revolted against the government. During this rebellion, many of the tribes, who agreed to join the labour corps, took shelter at Chingmeirong in camps provided by the State government to protect them from Kuki depredations. Rajendra Singh, in his study of the Anal communities, reports that "there was a case where the chief of Duthang Anal village appealed to the concerned government that the Anals are not Kukis and that they would not participate in Kuki rebellion" (Singh, 1981:13-14).

In the last many years, the sense of being a Naga has led many of the Naga tribes to come together under one umbrella. In their pursuit for the integration of the Naga ancestral homeland, many individuals from the Chandel Naga tribes have taken active roles in their own capacities for the cause. (Late) Ng. Mono Monsang from the present Changning village is one important figure in this regard. He was also one of the founder members of the Naga Integration Committee, Manipur and served as its President in 1970, and Rishang Keishing, a Tangkhul Naga (and former Chief Minister of Manipur), became the General Secretary.

Chandel Nagas were also one of the worst affected areas during the communal conflict between the Naga-Kuki conflicts in Manipur during the early 1990s. Many villages were burnt and thousands of people became homeless because of the conflict between the above two groups. Chandel district was one of the worst affected areas. Some Naga villages, particularly of Anal and Lamkang Nagas, situated on the periphery of the Chandel district, were affected badly during the conflict. Some of the worst affected Anal villages under the Chandel Chakpikarong sub-division include Shalluk, Bethel, Gilngai, Kanan, Kana Khubung, Warkhu, Dutejol, Kollen etc. Leaving behind their villages, paddy and jhum-fields, most of them became destitutes. In the present context, even though the tension between the two groups has come down relatively and the situation appears to be normal, however, many are not in a position to reclaim the land that originally belonged to them.

Christianity and Education in Identity Formation

The coming of Christianity in Monsang and the neighbouring villages in the 1920s opened a new vista for asserting their identity through education. Many people were converted to Christianity because of education. In the context of the Monsang Nagas, it was by the early 1970s that interests in the study of their tribe came to be felt by some of the educated persons within the tribe. This endeavour can be linked to the impact of education on the community, particularly in the post-Independence period. Egbert Khartu, the first Monsang graduate in 1966 (Roland, 2008:4) was one among those, who developed a deep interest in the study of his own community. Indeed, the formation of the *Monsang Historical and Customary Research Committee* in the mid-1970s for recording and preserving the history and culture of the tribe was the result of this awakening/consciousness among the Monsang educated citizens.

Through the initiative of the *Monsang Historical and Customary Research Committee,* a five-day seminar was organized in June 1977, held at present Liwa Changning village by inviting elders from all Monsang villages. The significance of the seminar lies in the publication of a small booklet, entitled *The Glimpses of the Monsang Culture and History*, in January 1978, by the *Monsang Historical and Customary Research Committee.* Another significance of the seminar worthy of note, as noted in the title of the booklet, was the participation of the prodigious Monsang folk singers. The perceptions shared by the old people, regarding the origin theory, migration, settlement and movement of the Sirtis (now Monsang) from place to place were cross-checked with the narrations in the folksongs. This suggests that historian's craft was very much employed while trying to derive history through the process of cross-checking folktales and folksongs. The booklet has a few collections of the Monsang folksongs. Interestingly, this small monograph has two sets of translations in it, one in Manipuri in the Bengali script by Egbert Khartu, and the other in English by R.K. Ranjit Singh. The revised edition of the English version was published in January 2011 by the same author. However brief and incomplete it may be, this small monograph remains to be a primary source for any beginner interested in the study of Monsang Naga history.

From the later part of the 1970s onwards, research and writing on the Monsang Naga tribe gradually increased. R.K. Ranjit Singh was the first non-native to study the Monsang community for his doctoral thesis. In his research on the tribe, he dealt with various aspects related to the Monsang Nagas – their society, economy, religion, and village government. His main focus lies on the emerging identity-orientation of 'this small group', in the post-Independence period. It is an intensive work considering the limitation of sources for the study and the time period it took to complete the study. Among the natives, Oliver Monsang was the first to undertake a research on the tribe. His research work, entitled, *Monsangs: A Social and Political Study*, reflects on the social life of the Monsangs, their traditional political system and developments in the recent decades. After him, for about two decades, there was no follow-up in the study of the Monsang tribe by natives or non-natives, except for the submission of Singh's Ph.D. thesis in 1985.

In recent years, writings on the Monsang Nagas have begun to emerge, particularly among theological students studying in different theological colleges across the country. Most of their researches revolve around themes like conversion to Christianity and its impact on the lives of the Monsang Nagas. Ng. Molarhring Monsang's thesis for the degree of Master of Divinity is a pioneering work on the conversion of the Monsangs to Christianity. The study discusses the history of the coming of Christianity to the Monsang country and the nature of conversion among the Monsang Nagas. According to him, the nature of conversion among the Monsang Nagas was individual conversion rather than mass conversion. He argues that the reason for conversion entailed individual interests and inclinations towards the new religion despite obstacles and torture, such as ostracizing the converted families from the village settlement areas. Events such as this in certain cases led to the formation of new villages. A few other works in this genre of literature include Sh. Alani Monsang's *The Impact of Christianity on the Monsang Naga Tribe of Manipur in the Twentieth Century* and Th. Rockson Monsang's *The Impacts of Christianity on Monsang Nagas*. The former discusses as to how Christianity had an impact on the traditional Monsang religious life. He argues that the traditional religious beliefs and practices, which included animal sacrifices to the invisible deities and spirits, slowly died down after conversion to Christianity. Rockson Monsang reflects on how Christianity brought both positive as well as negative impacts on the Monsang community.

Monsang Pioneers in Education

Among the Monsangs, the present Changning village was the first village to convert to Christianity in 1924. Ng. Kobung, K. Angkaka, K. Kotheng and Sh. Mochung embraced Christianity while studying at Aimol Christian School at Aimol Leining Tampak near present Pallel (Roland, 1999:29). The sudden transformation of Changning villagers whereby they could sing hymns and choruses after their conversion to Christianity was believed to have inspired other Monsang villages. Here, it is evident that the ability to read and write by learning western education was one of the factors as to why some of the Monsang youths from other Monsang villages wanted to convert to Christianity. According to Egbert Khartu, "the desire of reading the Bible and of singing the gospel songs and church hymns became a pressing demand for education among the Monsang people in the wake of the advent of Christianity in the early thirties of the 20th century" (Khartu, 2006:41).

Indeed, the desire for education was the reason for sending children to missionary schools at home and outside. However, only a few children could get support for higher studies outside. Late Ng. Mono Monsang from the present Changning village was one among them. He started his early schooling at Liwa Changning Lower Primary School in 1928. In 1933, Mono Monsang left to pursue his studies further at Kangpokpi Middle English School from class III until he completed his class VI in 1936. In 1937, he left for Jorhat Mission High School Jorhat, Assam, and completed his high school in 1942. He continued his further studies at Cotton College in Gauhati. However, because of the Second World War disturbances, he returned home and began to serve as a school teacher and became actively involved in the spread of education in the area. Ng. Mono Monsang was a devout Baptist and took active part in religious and social causes in his early days. He was a prolific orator and a dynamic person in his approach to life. Besides his contribution in religious field, Mono Monsang is better known among the Monsangs and their neighbouring tribes for his role in politics at local, state and even national levels. Because of his education and association with the missionaries and leaders from other tribes and communities, his reputation as a capable leader was acknowledged (Roland, 2008:14). When the first election in Manipur to elect members to the Interim Council was held in 1948-49, Ng. Mono Monsang was elected as a member of the Legislative Assembly of Manipur from Chandel (then Tengnoupal) constituency. In 1973, when the first Autonomous Distrcit Council election was held, Mono Monsang was elected, and became the First Chairman of the Council (Roland, 2008:15).

The second Monsang to have passed the Matriculation in 1952 was the Late Rev. Th. Kotha Monsang. He completed his matriculation from Jorhat Christian High School and continued his study at the Eastern Theological College Jorhat and became the first Monsang to have passed G. Th. in 1955 (Roland, 2008:7). Later on, he became the first Field Director of South East Manipur Baptist Association (SEMBA). He also took the gospel to different areas in Manipur. In order to meet the need of having a Monsang Bible literature, Th. Kotha was appointed bible translator by Monsang Naga Baptist Churches Association (MNBCA). The progress of the translation of the New Testament (Holy Bible) was unfortunately hindered by his untimely death. The responsibility to complete the unfinished task was, therefore, handed over to Rev. W. Moses of Sarei village. The translation of New Testament in Monsang dialect was completed recently.

The Roman Catholic Mission Schools also play a vital role in the education of Monsang society. Rev. Ts. Dominic Lumon, the present Archbishop of Manipur, was a student and a product of Catholic Mission Schools. He is the first tribal Bishop from Manipur. He belonged to present Monsang Pantha village. Late Ts. Florence from Monsang Pantha village and Ts. Nirmala from new Meeleen village – the Monsang women pioneers in educational field were also the product of Catholic Convent Schools. This is not to say that all these are the result of Christian Mission institutions alone. The point is to lay emphasis upon the light of education and the impact it has on Monsang community through the Christian schools and teachings.

Christianity has also impacted on language and literature. The spread of Christianity and education and the use of English as a medium of instruction reduced the linguistic diversity of different groups. The Monsang community also in due course began to write their own literature using Roman script. As far as Christian literature is concerned, the first Monsang Praise and Worship hymnal, known as '*Thangpa Jesu Minpaana Lha*', came out in 1998, published by the Monsang Naga Baptist Churches Association (MNBCA), Manipur. The Monsang New Testament ('*Ethar Ttongdeen*'), published by the Bible Society of India, was released at Japhou village in early 2010. The Monsang Catholic Churches have also come up with a praise and worship hymnal, titled "*Thangnhang Thamna Di Le Lha*", published by Monsang Catholic Liturgical Committee in 2006. There are also of lately gospel and love songs composed using Roman script as the medium of transmission.

The Need for Re-Defining Education

Modern education in Chandel as mention elsewhere is devoid of qualitative institutions and systematic systems of learning. Sadly, in the whole of Chandel district, there are only two higher secondary schools – the Maha Union Government Higher Secondary School Japhou, and Moreh Higher Secondary School. Yet the appointment of teachers and classes on regular basis is not carried out properly. There are also private tiny tots and schools mushrooming in the last few years. However, there is a need to reform the syllabus, infrastructure, recruitment processes, teachers' training programmes, teaching-method and the integrity of schools.

Well-qualified, devoted and sincere teachers are needed if educational institutions are to become a sanctuary of meaningful learning and engaging experience. Reformation in traditional methods of teaching-learning is required. Memorizing and vomiting out lessons do not actually help students exploit their potentials and realize their talents. Keeping abreast with the changing times, schools should incorporate an interesting blend of academia and extracurricular activities that can help equip the younger generations with much-needed skills. As every child/student is unique in his/her own ways and gifted with different talents, we need to groom and nurture them accordingly and make them realize who they are and what they want to be in life. Therefore, focus should be laid on rich curriculum that goes beyond conventional classroom teachings. Organizing seminars and workshops on diverse issues, talent hunt competitions and outdoor activities for students are indispensable in nurturing them for a brighter future of the nation. Above all, we need to inculcate in the minds of the students, religious, ethics and social values, something that is fading away.

References

Brown, R., 1873. *Statistical Account of the Native State of Manipur and Hill Territory under its Rule*. Delhi: Sanskaran Prakashan.

Dun, E.W., 1981. *Gazetteer of Manipur*. Delhi: Vivek Publishing Company (first published in 1886 by the Superintendent Government Printing, Calcutta under the orders of the Quarter-Master General in India).

Eaton, M. Richard, 1984. "Conversion to Christianity among the Nagas, 1876-1971." *Indian Economic and Social History Review* XXI (1): 1-44.

Elwin, Verrier (ed.), 1969. *The Nagas in the Nineteenth Century*. Bombay: Oxford University Press.

Grierson, G. A., 1904. *Linguistic Survey of India*. Vol. III, Part III.

Hodson, T.C., 1911. *The Naga Tribes of Manipur*. Delhi: Low Price Publications.

Horam, M., 1975. *Naga Polity*. New Delhi: B.R. Publishing Company.

Horam, M., 1977. *Social and Cultural Life of Nagas (The Tangkhul Nagas)*. Delhi: B.R. Publishing Corporation.

Loveson, Kh., 2006. *Souvenir of the Sirti Thiimjiitam Sourkhe (Monsang Naga Students' Union) Golden Jubilee (1956-2006)*, published by Sirti Thiimjiitam Sourkhe.

Kabui, Gangmumei, 1985. *Anal: A Trans-Border Tribe of Manipur*. Delhi: Mittal Publications.

Kabui, Gangmumei, 1991. *History of Manipur.* Vol. 1 (Pre-colonial period), New Delhi: National Publishing House.

Kamkhenthang, H., 1982. *Folk-Tales of Monsang-Moyon Tribe*. Directorate for the Development of Tribals and Backward Classes, Imphal: Government of Manipur.

McCulloch, Colonel, 1859. *Account of the Valley of Munnipore, and of the Hill Tribes, with a Comparative Vocabulary of the Munnipore and other Languages*, Calcutta.

Monsang, Alani Sh., 2004. *The Impact of Christianity on the Monsang Naga Tribe of Manipur in the Twentieth Century*. Unpublished thesis submitted to the Senate of Serampore College in partial fulfilment of the degree of Bachelor of Divinity, Gospel for Asia Biblical Seminary, Tiruvalla.

Monsang, Molarhring Ng., 2003. *The History of Christianity among Monsang Naga Tribe in Manipur: A Critical Study of the Dubious Understanding of their Conversion*. Unpublished thesis submitted in partial fulfilment of the requirements for the degree of Master of Divinity, Church on the Rock Theological Seminary, Andhra Pradesh.

Monsang, Oliver Th., 1982. *Monsangs: A Social and Political Study*. Unpublished dissertation submitted in partial fulfilment of the requirement for the Degree of Master of Arts, Division of Political Science, Jawaharlal Nehru University, Centre of Post-Graduate Studies, Imphal, Manipur.

Monsang, Rockson Th., 2004. *The Impacts of Christianity on Monsang Nagas*. Unpublished thesis submitted to the Senate of Serampore College in Partial fulfilment of the requirement toward the Degree of Divinity, Eastern Theological College Jorhat Assam.

Monsang Prominent Personalities: 2008. A Profile published by Sirti Upa Ruh (Monsang Tribe Union, Japhou.

Pemberton, R.B., 1968. *The Eastern Frontier of British India*. Guwahati.

Roland, Ng. and John, Kh., 1999. *Souvenir: Liwa-Changning Baptist Church Platinum Jubilee Celebration (1924-1999)*. Liwa-Changning Baptist Church, Chandel, Manipur.

Roy-Burman B.K., 1994. *Tribes in Perspective*. Delhi: Mittal Publications.

Shakespear, J., 1912. *The Lushai Kuki Clans*. Aizawl: Tribal Research Institute Aizawl, Mizoram.

Shimmi, Roland Y.L., 1988. *Comparative History of the Nagas: From Ancient Period till 1826*. New Delhi: Inter-India Publications.

Shimray, R.R., 1985. *Origin and Culture of Nagas*. New Delhi: Samsok Publications.

Singh, Joychandra L. (ed.), 1995. *The Lost Kingdom (Royal Chronicle of Manipur)*. Imphal: Prajanat Publishing House.

Singh, K.S. (ed.), 1998. *People of India: Anthropological Survey of India*. Vol. XXXI, Calcutta: Seagull Publications.

Singh, L. Iboongohal, 1967. *Cheitharol Kumbaba*. Imphal: Manipur Sahitya Parisad.

Singh, Rajendra, 1981. *The Anals of Manipur*. Imphal: Directorate for Welfare of Tribals and Backward Classes Manipur.

Singh, Ranjit R.K., 1985. *The Monsang Tribe of Manipur: A Study in Changing Orientation of a Small Group*. Unpublished thesis submitted for the Doctor of Philosophy in Anthropology in Dibrugarh University, Assam.

Steward, Lieutenant, 1955. "Notes on the Northern Cachar." *Journal of the Asiatic Society of Bengal* XXIV: 180-195.

Tohring, S.R., 2001. *The Identity of Pakans*. Unpublished dissertation submitted to Jawaharlal Nehru University in partial fulfilment of the requirements for the award of the Degree of Master of Philosophy.

Xaxa, Virginius, 2003. "Tribes in India" in *The Oxford India Companion to Sociology and Social Anthropology* (Veena Das, Ed.), pp. 373-408. New Delhi: Oxford University Press.

13

Traditional Forest Management through Indigenous Knowledge and Practices in Northeast India

A Case Study in Tangkhul Community, Manipur

Franky Varah and *T. Shimrah*

Forest biodiversity is being lost at an alarming rate, more so, in tropical and sub-tropical regions of the world. There have been many reports suggesting that species are presently being lost together with their tropical forest habitats (IUCN 2004; MEA, 2005). Globally, over half of the temperate broadleaf and mixed forest biome and nearly one quarter of the tropical rain forest biome have been fragmented or removed by humans (SCBD 2008). Managing forest biodiversity is, therefore, considered as top priorities for the long-term and broad flow of forest ecosystem services. Over the past few decades, more attention has been paid to the potential and real benefits regarding the use of indigenous knowledge (IK) in forest biodiversity management through sustainable utilization of forest resources (Berkes, 1999; Alcorn 1993; Gadgil *et al.* 1993) in one hand, and promotion of livelihood of local communities on the other as a win-win formula. Recently, many international organizations and conventions, including the World Commission on Environment and Development (WCED), Convention on Biological Diversity (CBD), Agenda 21, and Guiding Principles on Forests, specifically recognize the importance of indigenous knowledge as effective tools in augmenting the conservation of forest ecosystem. For example, indigenous territories encompass not more than 22 per cent of the world's land surface, but the areas hold about 80 per cent of its biodiversity (WRI, IUCN, UNEP 1991).

Further, the Government of India, through satellite image interpretation reported that the tribal areas in the Northeast India and areas of forest cover found a close correlation in terms of forest conservation (FSI, 2011). These two diversities are mutually supportive and reinforcing, thereby indicating that the relationship may not be accidental because many indigenous people's resource use and practice tend to conserve forest biodiversity, as they rely on the collection of resources from the forest for their livelihood, rather than converting these resources into commercial commodities. Nevertheless, the forest biodiversity is declining in these areas, which can be attributed to factors not related to traditional or indigenous knowledge system, such as population pressure, infrastructure development, market availability and climate change.

Over the last few decades, increasing cases of environment degradation and poverty have become areas of serious concern in the Northeast Indian region. Hilly areas of this region have an alarming range of development problems, such as food deficit, energy shortage, population growth, unemployment and declining agricultural productivity. Scarcity of resources and growing frequency of natural calamities have adversely affected the livelihood of the tribal people of the region. The developmental and environmental problems of the region originate in some of the most basic social, economic, political, cultural and historical features of the society: such as the loss of cultural identity and spiritual value, customary laws and the use of local knowledge. The challenges and opportunities that hilly areas are facing in transformation from subsistence to a market oriented economy are various, complex, and difficult. Livelihood strategies with other cultures have been very rapid and abrupt and this has led to complete disintegration of traditional and biodiversity management system in the region. It is important to realize that the study on the challenges and opportunities of indigenous knowledge based forest management are significant to sustain the livelihood of the tribal society in this region.

Objectives and Methodology

This paper is an attempt to understand the role of indigenous knowledge in forest management in contemporary India. It is structured in three parts: firstly, attempting to understand their knowledge about forests management and governance and its cultural significance exemplified as a major component and reflection of indigenous knowledge. Secondly, highlight the dilemmas and difficult situations faced by Tangkhuls in relation to nature conservation and forest biodiversity protection within a contested environment created by the processes of economic development and social change. Finally, the implications of these extensions and evaluation on what constitutes a pluralistic knowledge system of the environment will be discussed in terms of management strategies that can be used to promote the management of forest biodiversity in Ukhrul district.

A study was carried out during 2011-2012 to collect information on forest management in Ukhrul district. While collections on traditional forest management information have been gathered from the village chiefs, cultivators and elderly knowledgeable people through semi structured questionnaires, authors' own observation has also been reckoned with the answers they have provided. Further, challenges, strategies and measures needed to help conserve the Tangkhul culture and local forest biodiversity are also discussed.

Study Areas

Located at 23° 80'N - 25° 68' N latitude and 93° 03'E - 94° 78'E longitude with an area of 22,327 sq. km, the state of Manipur comprises 1820 sq. km of flat plateau of alluvial valley and 20,507 sq. km of hill territory. This mountain range forms a part of the Himalayan mountain system, which carries this cup-shaped wonderland inside its series of hill ranges. Manipur can be divided into two geo-topographical locations, i.e., Hill Districts and Imphal Plains. The total forest cover of Manipur is 76.54 per cent of which the hilly area covers 82 per cent and the valley, 13 per cent (FSI 2011). Manipur has two distinct socio-cultural groups: those living in the valley and those inhabiting the hills. According to the Census of India, 2011, people inhabiting the valley are predominantly from the Meitei's community (professing mostly Hinduism and Sanamahism as their religions), who comprise 1,628,224 persons (60% of the total population), while that of the hill are from various tribal groups (almost all are Christians), making up 1,093,532 (40% of the state's population) (Table 13.1).

Table 13.1: Manipur Forest Cover and Population (areas km^2)

Region	*Geographical Area (sq. km)*	*Population 2011*	*Total Forest Cover (areas in km^2)*
Manipur	22,327	27,21,756	17,090
Valley	2,238	16,28,224	352
Hill	20,089	10,93,532	16,738
Ukhrul	4,544	1,83,115	3,549

Source: FSI, 2011, Provisional Population Totals and data products and Census of India, 2011.

The Ukhrul district is part of the eastern Himalayan biodiversity hotspot, indicating its richness in biodiversity and high vulnerability to anthropogenic pressures. Over the past few decades, there has been a drastic increase in population, developmental activities, decrease in shifting cultivation cycle and the privatization of community forest for monoculture (horticulture crops and tea), which have increased the pressure on forests and their resources. These factors have also affected the livelihood base of the local poor, reinforcing persistent cycles of poverty amid 'plenty' in many pockets of the Ukhrul district.

Tangkhul Nagas

The Tangkhul is one of the Indigenous Naga tribe residing in Northeast India. They inhabit the biodiversity rich hills in the Ukhrul district of Manipur. They are the largest ethnic tribal people of Manipur with a population of 183,115 according to the 2011 Census. Being in the hilly area, their social and economic activities revolve around the village, land and forest, which form the basic foundation of their livelihood and culture. In Tangkhul tradition, one never abandons the concept of "my village, my home, and my clan". Their tradition reinforces this concept of ethno-territorialism. The village has been the highest political, social, economic and religious unit and the main source of spiritual, social and cultural bonding amongst the people.

The basic structure of governance in Tangkhul villages is a republic called the Village Authority (VA) known as *Hangvapam*. This *Hangvapam* is the highest institution in the village, which is responsible for a wide range of authority and governance such as judiciary, development, management of village lands, etc. The VA is headed by a hereditary chief called *Awunga*, with subordinate members, each of whom is called as *Hangvanao.* Each *Hangvanao* is representative of a clan, thus, ensuring that every clan is proportionately represented in the *Hangvapam.* All village festivals, social and religious functions begin with rites and scarifies by the *Awunga.* These customs and traditions bind together emotionally all members of the entire village community including the *Awunga.*

The Tangkhuls have rich reservoir of knowledge about management, utilization and conservation of nature and its resources, which is conceptualized as indigenous knowledge through various sacred rituals, cultural practices and beliefs in which they remain embodied. The traditional knowledge of the Tangkhul stems mainly from four sources: Firstly, the experience accumulated over centuries and transmitted from generation to generation. Secondly, the experiences shared socially by the members of the group. Thirdly, the experience shared in the household or the domestic group to which the individual belongs. And lastly, the personal experience, particular to each individual, achieved through the repetition of the annual cycles, enriched by the perceived variations and unpredictable conditions associated with them. Tangkhul indigenous knowledge is determined by a set of shared meanings available to individual knowledge.

Most of Tangkhul culture and customs and its traditions bonded the family, clan and the village as a community in the form of songs, folklores, proverbs, dances, value beliefs, rituals, agricultural practices, stone sculptures, wood carvings, and designs on clothes. Most of this teaching and learning process took place at the Morung (learning and socializing dormitories) and also during celebration of festivals and agricultural work, where knowledge was shared by ways of daily activities. Most of the folk songs speak about or relate to the historical background of the Tangkhul community, the village, the clan, and certain well known individuals. Seasonal songs are sung only in their particular season as a matter of relevance. For instance, spring songs inform what the spring season is and what one should be doing during that season. There is at least one folk song for each period of the agricultural cycle. Oral historical traditions have been the primary means of passing village, clan and individual story, where knowledgeable elder narrates the customs and traditions of the past. They also share about spirit worship.

Traditional Livelihood Strategies

The Tangkhuls largely depend on forest resources for their livelihood and the mode of utilization is of subsistence. Agriculture, hunting, fishing, and food gathering are important activities of their sustenance. The inherent indigenous knowledge system allows them to interact with the surrounding forests in different ways. They use their indigenous knowledge base to produce for their daily needs and other purposes, which apparently prove the values and significance of forest biodiversity in their way of life. The linkages of forests with livelihood, food security, and agriculture make it very important. Non-timber forest products (NTFPs) from forest biodiversity, such as herbs, medicine plants, fibre, honey, gum, nuts, fruits, flowers, seeds and wild meat are essential food items used by the Tangkhuls to sustain their way of life. Bamboo and canes have multidimensional values such as furniture, weapons (bows and arrows, bamboo spears, etc.), construction material for houses, huts and fence and bamboo as food item. The culture and religious and traditional perception of forest biodiversity also includes those plants and animals connected to their beliefs (nature worship) and traditional rituals. Some plants and animals have special usage in the Tangkhul culture; for example, a special type of small bamboo with long internodes is used for drinking rice beer from a common pot, feathers of the hornbill bird is used to decorate the headgears. Further, a dance form has been evolved, inspired by the hornbill and to this day, the hornbill is widely respected in the Tangkhul culture.

In the Tangkhul traditional practice, trees such as oak and alder are never cut or uprooted completely. They are either lopped or pruned in order to ensure continuity of its survival. The point at which the tree is to be lopped requires clear ecological and physiological knowledge, which comes from elders through practice. It is lopped about 15-20 cm above the node at the breast height or just above it. The clear trunks (without node at reachable distance from ground) are usually not lopped; rather they are pruned. When the coppices are about one-two years old, each of which attaining a minimum girth size of about 25cm, then they are lopped leaving the smaller coppices and as such the productivity of fuel wood is enhanced with shorter period of time. The smaller remaining coppices grow fast and in the subsequent year, they can be harvested, thus one can collect fuel wood almost every year until the life span of that tree. The process of lopping provides other services, such as cleaning of invasive alien species, undesirable weeds and also protection from forest fire.

Shifting Agriculture as a Way of Life

Shifting cultivation is the major occupation of the Tangkhul Nagas. The practice of shifting cultivation represents an intricate relationship between ecology, economy, society and the cultural ethos of the region. There is often no clear cut demarcation of forest and agricultural lands. In shifting cultivation areas, the same piece of land can be under cultivation at one time and regeneration of forest at another point of time. While clearing the cultivation field, certain plants such as Alder trees are spared, which are good for soil conservation.[1] As opposed to the general notion, the Tangkhuls believe that shifting cultivation helps the forest to regenerate on its own and gives rise to new plantations from time to time and contributes to conservation through a number of practices, including the use of more variety of plant species than other agriculture and food production system. Further, shifting cultivation produces many kinds of food, which are organic in nature. For example, the farmer produces a wide range of mixed cropping and sequential harvesting in the jhum field. This multiple cropping system creates agro-biodiversity and makes gene pool conservation possible, which is absent in other agriculture system. Different age of the fallow forest provide different products for livelihood. This richness of biodiversity is possible with the knowledge and effort developed and evolved by shifting cultivators over centuries.

The conservation practices of the Tangkhuls are deeply interwoven in their day to day lifestyle, and forest related livelihood pursuits of their understanding of the environment practice and act as a mode of cultural conservation. Every person has an equal share, and each member of the society plays a role according to his physical and mental abilities. For example, at the time of selection of site for the shifting cultivation, religious ceremonies are performed by the elderly and experienced members of the community, while the felling of trees and clearing of jungles as well as burning of the dried biomass is carried out by the younger members of the village community. At least one tree in the middle of the field is left standing as a refuge for the tree spirit. Whether the shifting agricultural field is located in private land or community lands, it is always in one's mind as an obligatory responsibility to strike a balance between meeting their present needs while protecting the environment for future generations. Using their indigenous knowledge for controlling the menace of diseases, some of the traditional farmers alter certain crops and plants as biological control measure, adjust crop density, plan for suitable time of planting, mulching, multiple cropping, planting without tillage or minimum tillage, rotation of crops, etc. For example, rice is mixed with other crops primarily to make a physical barrier for the movement of insect pests-pathogens. From time to time, creeping vegetables like pumpkin, cucumber, etc., are included in between plants primarily for checking the weed pests to attract the insect's pest pathogen for feeding in preference over the rice crop.

Belief System Facilitates Forest Conservation

The Tangkhuls believe that nature is endowed with spirits; benevolent and malevolent spirits. They believe in the existence of the creator called *Ameowo*, who is a benevolent spirit. It was widely believed that the creator, through a benevolent entity, has little concern with humanity. The malevolent spirit had more to do with people' lives inhabiting every stream, mountain and forest to bring about upon men illness and misfortune. The Tangkhuls were in constant endeavour to appease their spirit embodied in huge rocks, caves, forests, rivers, and every place one can think of. The appeasing of the sacred is connected with environment protection. They believed that if they can protect the spirit/sacred tree well, then it will protect the village and wildlife of the forest, and bring rain and provide general protection of the environment and bring good luck and fortune. Besides, forests were believed to be the abodes of the spirits. For example, in Tangkhul tradition, there are numerous festivities associated with erecting monoliths (totem) either wooden or stone, among them, maximum importance was given to *Marankasa* (feast of merits), erecting wooden pillars as symbol of honour, dignity and prosperity. There was an elaborate ritual involved in the selection of the tree to be used as pillar, for the actual carving and transportation of the pillar, and for its erection and dedication. Before the tree is cut, the priest propitiates the spirit of the tree by offering rice beer, sacrificing animals and other food items as offerings to the guardian spirits. Trees are respected as they are believed to belong to forest spirits. Such belief gives them the conscience that they cannot take more than they need. This implies that the fear of the spirits is the most effective means of social control. For instance, sites like Shirui Kashong (Shirui Peak) are considered sacred and as such they look upon this peak with respect, fear and wonder.[2]

Further, the Tangkhul Naga established a system of beliefs and taboos for forest conservation and management practices that ensured the existence of forests even in critical and fragile areas by developing and adopting mechanisms, like placing certain taboos on harvesting, prohibition on hunting of particular animal species within specific area and also during specific periods to ensure the continuance of animal life. Culture and religion played an important role in developing, managing and protecting natural biodiversity and common resources. The Tangkhul society succeeded in managing resources well over time by adopting traditional practices, such as religion and ritual representation management. The key point is not religion per se, but the use of emotionally powerful cultural symbols to a particular moral code and management system. For example, a piece of cloth is woven around the trunk of some flowering trees like Papaya (*Carica papaya*), Yongchak (monkey tree/*Parkiaroxbughii*) and Tera trees (*Bombaxceiba*), as a gesture of protecting the modesty of the tree and to increase fertility so as to get more yield, which otherwise may stop bearing fruits. However, the logic behind is that the bright coloured clothes deter the pest from attacking the roots and stems of the trees, which affect their flowering abilities. The application of indigenous knowledge in the management of natural resources has developed into a systematic body of knowledge with regard to management of natural environment, functioning of the ecosystem and habitat of human use in a more holistic way without damaging the natural process and cycle.

Regulations on Forest Use

The structure of land systems varies from village to village. All the tribes affirm that the land is the source of life and is sacred. They do not think of the land and all the things in it as being inanimate objects, but regard them as having life and power in themselves, so the land is the basis of life and unity. As mentioned above, like most of the indigenous communities, Tangkhuls have a deep sentimental attachment and socio-cultural orientation towards the land on which they lived. This attachment renders to both individuals and to the community as a whole, a sense of belonging to land. It is an important social and cultural phenomenon because it is deeply rooted in their homestead, landed property, relatives, clan and community in general.

However, a closer look at the oral account handed down by the forefathers shows an interesting insight. There was no uniformity regarding landholding system among the Tangkhuls; there were slight variances. The local community was allowed unrestricted accessibility by considering the forests as common property of the village. For them, some of the main important products of the forest were timber and fuel wood. The owner of a piece of forest in private lands can extract as much trees for timber or fuel wood or any other requirements. Mutual help and concern for fellow villagers is inherent in Tangkhul community. The sharing of forest products among the community was prevalent irrespective of the economic status of the individual. For instance, in a situation where a person is facing shortage of timber in his forest land, he would request his near and close relative/s or friend/s for permission to extract timber from his forest, which is generally granted considering the health and amount of required timbers. However, such help was limited to construction of one's house only; not for commercial use. In the absence of proper market facilities and healthcare systems, till now, activities such as collection of non-timber forest products (NTFP) and hunting in the forest lands do not have boundary or ownership restriction since it is customary and essential part of life of tribal community to rely on forest for wild animals as their protein source and also wild medicinal plants for their local healthcare system. Sustainable use of such forest biodiversity is essential for the subsistence and also for the cultural and spiritual identity of Tangkhuls.

Across the villages in Tangkhul community, land resources were managed and owned in such a way that every family had access to resources required to meet their needs. Economic interest and development was dictated by one's needs and not by commercial interests or greed. Land resource allocation was done according to equitable identification of factors, such as the needs of a family or individual and their ability to utilize their allocated land. Till now, it is common in all villages to have substantial area of forest lands as community land or village land in which no individual member of the village has claim of ownership. This area of land is maintained with a clear consciousness that in the event when certain members of community may face scarcity of land, they can utilize this community land subject to their requirements limited to subsistent level. It is this wisdom that ensures that no one in the Tangkhul community is considered landless. Redistribution of land among those, who need more and who require less was a common practice. This is an efficient system in handling poverty and food security in villages where the community is left alone with no support services. Therefore, it is necessary to have a good understanding of the land system and the mechanism of its operation. Proper land use is probably the best conservation practice.

The Tangkhuls have a tradition of erecting monoliths (totems) and on such occasions, a series of feasting was conducted for the village. Such activities, although generally done by richer members of communities, have social obligation and help in coherence and strengthen the bond of community existence of the tribal community. By organizing feasting for all villagers, irrespective of social status, gender and age, better co-ordination, understanding and affection towards one another are brought about. Moreover, at the time of feasting, more traditional knowledge is passed on from elders to younger members of community by way of songs, dances and stories.

Some examples of land use and forest management in the farming systems commonly practised in the region are contour cultivation, mulching, hedgerow planting, inter cropping, rotation, and minimum tillage. These are relatively simple to apply and are likely to increase crop yield as well as protect from soil erosion and forest degradation.

Challenges of Forest Management: new development

No doubt, with rapid increase in population, along with better market facilities, the Tangkhul community is not alien to various problems and challenges that the forest-user groups face in managing forests. The Tangkhul traditional outlook, customs, beliefs, rituals, concept of forest biodiversity conservation have been subjected to aggressive changes due to the impact of socio-economic, cultural and political forces, which are also responsible for the breakup of traditional Tangkhul society. The Tangkhuls are no longer living in conditions of balanced ecosystems that they managed and maintained earlier. Such alteration gives rise to new needs and values, which may imply the loss of indigenous knowledge, the shattering of old binds and beliefs, which have been the pillar of social cohesion and cultural continuity. During the last couple of decades, there are internal challenges within the Tangkhul community that can be attributed to socio-economic transition, population dynamics as well as the influence of globalisation and internal transformation in the Tangkhul society.

Today the Tangkhul Nagas are predominantly Christian, forming more than 90 per cent of the population. Colonialism and missionaries were the first, who forbade the Tangkhul converts from taking part in festivals, dances, singing folk songs and other Tangkhul customs. For example, Christian beliefs forbade worshiping traditional sacred objects and such prohibition slowly resulted into change in their relationship with nature. Christian priests tend to be relentless and demanded destruction of such sacred objects. These attitudes not only undermined the priceless values of people's culture, but also resulted in total chaos and confusion for some generations. The present cause of forest biodiversity crises are often expressions of cultural crises, arising from loss of traditional and cultural roots without acquiring new roots.

Anti-tribal Land Laws Extension to the Hill

Today, there are broadly two property systems, based on ethnic features that govern land rights in Manipur. Each system has its own enforcement mechanisms as well as codification of rules and norms. The first system of property rights prevails in the hill, where community ownership governed by unwritten customs and traditions of the village administration exercises executive, judiciary and administrative autonomy. Despite absence of land records in the hill area, it is in principle agreement and practice that there is no government land in the tribal inhabited hill areas and, as such, the villagers hold the land with the sanction of the chief and community, but not by the state government. However, the second system of property rights is prevalent in the valley, where complete private individual ownership exists and is protected by the state through its laws and institutions.

Thus, the land tenure in Manipur is a combination of community and private ownership of land. Legal processes in Manipur state have introduced changes in the land laws and its extension to the hill region was first made in 1956 through the Manipur Hill Village Authority Act. The Act determines the number of members of the village authorities on the basis of the number of taxpaying houses. The Act defined the strength of the village authorities. The Act also put certain limitations on the position and power of the village chief. For instance, according to these Acts, the elections of chairman was introduced and the traditional chief, who is respected and revered by the tribal communities, is demoted to ex-official position. In fact, such Acts countermand the age old traditional tribal institutions, thereby infringing on the time tested customary laws. Again, an attempt was made in 1967 to strip the chiefs' rights by passing the Manipur Hill Areas Acquisition of Chief's Rights Act, 1967,' by paying compensation. Mention may be made here that while global communities have recognized and appreciated the relevance and effectiveness of indigenous knowledge in the management and conservation of resources, especially forest management, the state of Manipur has been busy making deliberate attempts to sabotage such intact tribal customary laws of forest management. Despite vehement opposition from various tribal groups of Manipur as well as from the

Hill Areas Committee, the Manipur Legislative assembly passed this Act (Shimray, 2006).

Further, the state attempts to expand its control and influence in the hill areas under Manipur Land Reforms and Land Revenues Act, 1960 (MLR and LRA). In the latest proposal, sub-section (2) of section 1, the phrase "except the hill areas thereof" was to be changed to: "it extends to the whole of the state of Manipur". The desirability of a single law is given as the official reason. On the other hand, from the perspective of the hill people, this Act is meant to facilitate the transfer of tribal land in the areas to the predominantly non-tribal inhabitants of the Imphal valley. Our understanding is that the blanket application of the Act to all parts of the state in its present form will create forest management problematic without achieving the stated objectives; thus, exposing the hill people to the risk and threat of losing their land without creating an alternative livelihood system.

State Policies

Central government and state are developing various policies and laws related to natural resource management. Laws and policies have played an important part in the process of legitimisation of state's control over the land and forest of the tribes in Manipur through Joint Forest Management (JFM); attempt to declare protected areas and the creation of wildlife department. There has been frequent clash of interest between the indigenous tribal communities and state government regarding the management of forest. In Ukhrul district, the examination of the implementation of Manipur state forest policy brings out this fact. Social Forestry and JFM are the two important programmes closely associated with the forest policy in Ukhrul district.

Social Forestry: According to the government report, social forestry is often suggested as a solution to the problem of deforestation. This view is strongly contested by local community (*see* Box 14.1). The crisis of Indian forests results from the decision taken to promote the expansion of produce of the forest, including meeting the fuel wood, fodder and small timber requirement of the local people from the nearby areas, which left the forests unable to maintain the ecological balance. The social forestry programme was

Box 13.1

The present field work indicates that the goals of this programme have not been attained by the project. Unfortunately, indications are that most of these objectives have not been attained by the social forestry programme as implemented in the Ukhrul district. Interviews with some of the farmers involved in the programmes at Halang village in Ukhrul district explain that under the social forestry programmes, the eucalyptus trees cause major disturbance to ecosystem. In already water-scarce village like Halang, these trees drain away most of the water thereby adversely affecting the water table, and rendering terrace agriculture on the neighbouring lands impossible; further, it leads to a decline in soil fertility as most of the nutrients are absorbed by this tree; this is because it is a fast growing tree and absorbs a lot of nutrients and water from the soil. Since eucalyptus is an alien species, the introduction of this species drives away native species. This affects the biodiversity of the landscape.

aimed at combining fast growing species for village timber and fuel wood needs with fruit and other species that are required for the village economy. It was also meant to involve the local population in their own development; by making them a part of the scheme that was to be implemented in degraded forests and waste lands.

Joint Forest Management: The government of India circular issued in June 1990 to all the states and union territories provided guidelines for the involvement of village communities and voluntary agencies in the regeneration of degraded forests, which is known as Joint Forest Management (JFM). JFM, which has taken off in a big way in many states in the country, is still at an initial stage in the region. The idea of JFM implies the handing over of certain rights to village communities to appropriate natural resources for their own use. However, there is a lack of clear definition of who precisely are the right holders and what are the kind of rights and sanctions that can be applied, which impeded the process of establishing social institutions. An important obstruction to the full development of JFM is that the people have been involved in protection, but have not been given enough authority to deal with management. Due to lack of clarity regarding tenure, the villages are often apprehensive of their future status.

The major issues with the forests are what returns can be guaranteed to the communities to generate sustained interest in their protection. If the forests are in good condition, nearby communities probably have already been getting the benefit from the non-timber forest products. For instance, in Ukhrul, the forest department's effort to introduce or expand JFM programmes in village forests that are listed as unclassed forests have not been well appreciated by the communities. While the communities consider that all the so-called unclassed forest areas are effectively under the community-controlled forests, the government's efforts to introduce JFM in such areas for better forestry development and management have been resented by the communities as government's ploy to control the community forests.

Opportunities of Forest Management Strategies

In recent years, the Tangkhuls are making several efforts to protect and revive traditional institutions either in the traditional form, or innovative forms, in order to empower local communities with appropriate information, skills and technologies to respond in their own way to the threat posed by various forces. For example, many villages have created a new system as Village Development Authority (VDA). The village chief takes care of land and forest issues and also safeguards the village customary laws, while the VDA look after development issues and takes care of all government schemes and its beneficiaries. Conservation initiatives must result in tangible social, environmental, and economic benefits to communities. The significance of indigenous knowledge as a mechanism to implement management partnership and self-government and as a mechanism to integrate local values into decision making can be best appreciated in this context. These measures would act to strengthen their local knowledge of forest management wherever it still exists together with community's property management system to sustain.

The Tangkhul people have largely preserved their identities, value of kinship, institutional reciprocity and knowledge and continue to resist alien resource exploitation and management onslaughts. Besides, their increasing awareness of natural resource management is stimulating their interest of rediscovering their traditional knowledge. In fact, the institutional values of self-management may have been reclaimed, re-conceptualized, and renegotiated among the Tangkhul people. One of the best examples of this process is the existence of the number of self-initiated institutions, like the Student Association (Tangkhul Katamnao Long) and youth organization (Tangkhul Mayar Ngala Long), which issue notices not to indulge in government related projects like tree plantation and other activities, which are likely to disturb the ecological balance. These institutions in collaboration with the All Tribals Students Union of Manipur (ATSUM) and Naga Students Federation (NSF) have successfully resisted such structural exploitation of the forest by the Manipur state government and raised awareness of biodiversity importance. They have tried to involve the participation of villagers in regeneration, protection, conservation and management of degraded forests. It seems that here is a deep disconnect between the interests of Tangkhul and the government and private agencies involved in participatory programmes like in JFM.

Keeping traditional ancestral domains, such as forests and natural resources under communal tenure is an effective strategy for maintaining forest management. The local people are more familiar with the given forest biodiversity. The future of forest management lies in such strategies, as does the well-being of the people of communities dependent on forests. The failure to ensure local co-operation in biodiversity conservation efforts may make the local people indifferent and perhaps even hostile to the effort because of the top down initiatives, which people might not be very receptive of. From the discussions with local people, it came out that the tribal people oppose any policy that treats every community as homogeneous or entails the enactment of a uniform law applicable to all without acknowledging the existence of traditional land owning system and also governance. Assimilation and integration are seen as attempts to undermine historical and customary rights over territory and natural resources. Any special protection accorded is seen by them as a legitimization of their distinct identity and a prelude to state formation of the tribal areas.

In the indigenous communities, land and forests are the two basic resources for subsistence. Therefore, from ages, their land and forest rights are carefully and dearly guarded, but very often this right is threatened with attempts to change land from communal ownership to state ownership, which have disrupted behavioural pattern, indigenous knowledge and social self-regulation mechanisms that once ensured the conservation of biodiversity as well as sustainable uses of species and ecosystem (Gadgil and Berkes, 1991; Gadgil and Guha 1992; Berkes 1999). Lack of security of land rights and user rights for communities is a major cause of decline in local systems of forest management. Biodiversity conservation measures should be incentivized to ensure the participation and ownership of stakeholder communities. Conservation measures should enhance local people's livelihoods, technical and management capacities, and decision-making role, otherwise sustainability can prove elusive.

Is it possible that indigenous knowledge based forest management can survive within a context where powerful actors, governments, international institutions in charge of globalizing an economic pattern of open markets and deregulation? Will we be aware enough to make the difference between genuine cases and those which are just a co-option to the prevailing model? There is no single model of community-based forest management, but all of them have as a common trait the necessary autonomy and sovereignty of their legitimate authorities in order to make decisions relevant to the control, use and management of the resource-base of the community with a view to fulfil the needs of its members. Hence, management partnerships for natural resources are best built upon existing social capital, such as indigenous knowledge and culture, traditional institutions, and customary rights and practices, from the community level up. By empowering and trusting these institutions and building their management capacity, the formal authorities created viable partners in the new biodiversity management system, which relies on networks of villages and community conserved areas. The best hope for conservation may come from the fusion of indigenous knowledge and science. In the past, wasteful and selfish exploitation of forests by individuals was prevented by a system of social control of the traditional institutions. But strong forces are today eroding Tangkhul traditional practice of forest conservation. Even in this bleak scenario, there is reason to hope for the re-institutionalization of self-management system.

Conclusions: How Different Worldviews Can Work Together

On the basis of what has been said above, it is possible to identify that the North Eastern Region of India is a rich tapestry of culture and biodiversity. Overwhelming biodiversity, heritage drawn from the ages and the presence of a large number of diverse groups makes this place a cultural and biodiversity hotspot. The study showed how the emergence and application of scientific knowledge has contributed to the decline of existing indigenous knowledge system with regard to forest management, and how such a shift has led to conservation and livelihood related challenges in the forest dependent Naga tribal communities of North Eastern India. Tangkhul's indigenous knowledge cannot stand solely viable in this modern age beneath population pressure and the constricting global market forces in Naga society. An attempt is also made to analyse the experience of social forestry and joint forest management in Ukhrul district that pointed towards some of the unsuccessful implementation efforts based on scientific forestry, which resulted into dwindling soil fertility and environmental degradation. Because the modern government is a relatively new force in the region, they are not always able to understand the environmental problems and the issues related to the ecosystem readily. Hence, it is important to involve the indigenous knowledge of the local people.

The present research shows an urgent need and consolidated use of pluralistic system of knowledge to solve the loss of forest biodiversity. This pluralism can include local knowledge about specific ecosystem as well as non-local perspective in interpreting that knowledge. There are different ways of knowing and no one standard for determining the validity of knowledge. This study suggests strategies to combine both the knowledge systems for management efficiency in order to achieve economic development, social change, and forest conservation. The systems that follow the principle of sustainable rural livelihoods must be recognized and strengthened with appropriate policy support to form the basis for sustainable forest management. This study proposes a framework, which may assist the environmental management challenges in Ukhrul.

1. To retain culturally significant element of traditional way of life, combining the old and the new in a way that it maintains and enhances their identity while allowing the Tangkhul society and economy to evolve. First and foremost, the Sixth Schedule and the Panchayati Raj Act should be extended and effectively implemented by the devolution of requisite finances and powers, in the hills and the valley, respectively. The decentralization must be accompanied by a provision for democratically elected local bodies with due representation for women. The Land Reforms Act should not be imposed on the hill people. A Land and forest Commission may be set up immediately to look into the issues of land and forest ownership in keeping with the ethnic diversity and territorial rights of the people.
2. In order to empower local communities with appropriate information, skills and technologies, efforts are made to protect and revive indigenous knowledge either in the traditional form or in new innovative forms. However, the government policy of conserving forest biodiversity in Ukhrul district is targeted more towards legitimizing its own governance rather than addressing the needs of the people. But government and outside agencies should not replace the local community's right to make decisions that affect their livelihood and culture. Instead, efforts should be made to assist the local people to preserve and utilize their indigenous knowledge and natural resources in order to protect biodiversity and sustain their traditional livelihood.
3. No doubt all indigenous knowledge system may not be scientific or may not be sustainable. But with necessary technical and scientific input, they contain ample scope, for formulating development alternatives with minimum risks or costs. For instance, Naga practice of offering protection to certain tree species (such as oak and alder) and also the widespread practice of shifting cultivation, which can be examined further. A regime of tree species protection blends with shifting cultivation, which is mainly based on clearing of trees. The fine balance and the many dynamics that may characterize this process may be interesting from an analytical

point of view of scientific knowledge. Keeping this in view, there is an urgent need to identify, document, and study such practices through proper research.

Notes

1. Jhum fields are often found intermingling with alder plant, which is a socially valued tree and Tangkhul farmers have recognized their significance since times immemorial. According to Ramakrishnan (2004), the scientific justification of keeping these plants intact is that it enriches the soil by fixing atmospheric nitrogen to the tune of 125 kg per hectare per year.
2. Shirui Kashong, which is now preserved as a national park, is known for its rich biodiversity and the flower that grows in this particular peak called the Shirui Lily is the State Flower of Manipur.

References

Alcorn J.B. 1993. Indigenous Peoples and Conservation, *Conservation Biology* 7: 424-426.

Berkes Fikret. 1999. Sacred Ecology: Traditional Ecological Knowledge and Resource Management, Landon, Braun-Brumfield.

Census of India, 2011. *Provisional Population Totals and Data Products: Census 2011: Manipur.*

Forest Survey of India. 2011, 2007, 2001. *India State of Forests Report,* Forest Survey of India, Dehradun.

Gadgil, Madhav, and Berkes, F. 1991. Traditional Resource Management Systems, *Resource Management and Optimization*, 18: 127-141.

Gadgil, Madhav, and Guha, R. 1992. *The Fissured Land: An Ecological History of India.* Oxford University Press. New Delhi.

Gadgil, Madhav, Berkes Fikret, and Folke Corlas 1993. Indigenous Knowledge for Biodiversity Conservation, *Ambio*, 22 (2-3): 151-155.

Hodson, T.C. 1911. *The Naga Tribes of Manipur.* London: Macmillan.

International Union for the Conservation of Nature (IUCN). 2004. 2004 IUCN red list of threatened species: A global species assessment. IUCN: Gland, Switzerland and Cambridge, UK.

Lungharwo, Thingreiphy. 2010. "Traditional Occupation and Livelihood Practice in Northeast India", in Tamayo, E. (eds) *Traditional Livelihood and Indigenous Peoples*, Asia Indigenous People Pact (AIPP): 85-106.

Millennium Ecosystem Assessment. 2005. Ecosystems and Human Well-Being: Policy Responses. Volume 3, Ch. 8. Island Press, Washington, DC.

SCBD. 2008. Subsidiary Body on Scientific, Technical and Technological Advice

(13/3). In-depth review of the expanded programme of work for forest biological diversity.

Shimray U.A. 2004. Land use System in Manipur Hills: A case study of the Tangkhul Naga, In Walter Fernandes, Sanjay B. (ed.) *Land, People and Politics: Contest over Tribal Land in Northeast India*, Guwahati: NESRC.

WRI, IUCN, UNEP 1991. *Caring for the Earth: A Strategy for Sustainable Living*. Gland, Switzerland: IUCN, UNEP and WWF.

Contributors

Dr. Victor Ahum, Ph.D. from Jawaharlal Nehru University, Independent Researcher

Mr. Maheishang Awungshi, Ph.D. Scholar, Manipur University

Dr. Ringkahao Horam, Assoc. Prof. and Head of Department, Political Science Department, Modern College, Manipur University, Imphal

Dr. Mess Jajo, Ph.D. from Jamia Millia Islamia, New Delhi, Independent Researcher

Mr. Yuimirin Kapai, Asst. Professor, Rajdhani College, University of Delhi, Delhi

Mr. A.C. Kharingpam, Asst. Professor, Jamia Millia Islamia, New Delhi

Mr. Somie Monsang, Asst. Professor, Miranda House, University of Delhi, Delhi

Dr. Tuisem Ngakang, Asst. Professor, Bharati College, University of Delhi, Delhi

Dr. Wonkhuimi Raman, Assoc. Professor and Head of Department, Education, DM College, Imphal

Mr. T. Shimrah, University School of Environment Management, GGS Indraprastha University, New Delhi.

Ms. Lucy Jajo Shimray, Assoc. Professor, DM College, Imphal

Dr. A.S. Shimreiwung, Asst. Professor, Tezpur University, Assam

Mr. Thodchuingam Shinglai, Ph.D. Scholar, Jawaharlal Nehru University, New Delhi

Mr. Franky Varah, Ph.D. Scholar, Jawaharlal Nehru University, New Delhi

Dr. A.S. Yaruingam, Head, Department of African Studies, Delhi University; President, Tangkhul Scholars' Association